FRAUD & DECEiT: HOW TO STOP BE

362.88
Suthers, John W.
Fraud and deceit

S966f

122462

FRAUD & DECEiT: HOW TO STOP BEING RIPPED OFF

by John W. Suthers
and Gary L. Shupp

ARCO PUBLISHING, INC.
NEW YORK

Published by Arco Publishing, Inc.
219 Park Avenue South, New York, N.Y. 10003

Copyright © 1982 by Arco Publishing, Inc.

All rights reserved. No part of this book may be reproduced, by any means, without permission in writing from the publisher, except by a reviewer who wishes to quote brief excerpts in connection with a review in a magazine or newspaper.

Library of Congress Cataloging in Publication Data

Suthers, John W.
  Fraud and deceit.

   1. Fraud. 2. Consumer protection.   I. Shupp, Gary L.   II. Title.
HV6695.S75   362.8'8   81-10841
ISBN 0-668-05318-6   AACR2

Printed in the United States of America

CONTENTS

Acknowledgments vii

Foreword ix

1 **Business Opportunity and Investment Frauds (The Deal of a Lifetime)** 1
Commodity Futures Fraud — Franchising and Vending Machine Frauds — Invention Marketing Frauds — Land Frauds — Ponzi Schemes — Pyramid Promotional Schemes — Raising Creatures Great and Small: For a Profit — Securities Fraud — Work-at-Home Schemes

2 **Merchandising Frauds (Things Aren't Always As They Appear To Be)** 21
Auto Sales Fraud — Bait and Switch Advertising — Contest Winners — Deceptive Pricing — Encyclopedias — Freezer Plans — The Funeral Industry — Going Out of Business Sales — Health Clubs — Home Solicitation Sales — Magazine Subscriptions — Mail Fraud — Unordered Merchandise (A Gift to You) — Vacation Frauds — Wholesale Buyer's Club

3 **Repair Frauds and Home Improvement Schemes (The Art of Compounding Your Problems)** 42
Automobile Repair Fraud — Energy Saving Frauds — Free Inspection Frauds — Home Repair Frauds — Swimming Pool Rackets — Television Repair Fraud

4 **Self-Improvement Schemes (Your Dreams Can Cost You Money)** 52
Body and Bosom Building Schemes — Dance Studio Rackets — Education Courses — Fortune-Telling Frauds — Song Sharks and Vanity Publishers — Talent Agency Frauds

5 **Charity Rackets and Frauds on the Sick or Elderly (Swindlers Have No Heart)** 62
Charity Rackets — Lonely Hearts Clubs — Medical Frauds — Religious Frauds

6 Commercial Fraud Schemes (Getting "The Business")   70
Advance Loan Fee Schemes — Bust-Outs and Bankruptcy Frauds — Check Fraud Schemes — Computer Crimes — Construction Fraud — Corporate Shell Games — Coupon Fraud — Credit Capers — Credit Card Fraud — Debt "Consolidation" and Debt Adjustment Frauds — Directory Advertising Frauds — Employment Agencies — False Billing Schemes — Insurance Fraud — Offshore Banks — Tax Shelter Frauds

7 Miscellaneous "Classic Cons"   98
Confidence Games — Missing Heir Scheme — Obituary Frauds — Pidgeon Drop

The Language of Fraud and Deceit   106

A Directory of Consumer Protection Agencies (Whom to Call When You're Suspicious or When You Haven't Been Suspicious Enough)   110

Acknowledgments

There are always long lists of persons whose assistance was invaluable in completing any project. But with this work there are two who cannot be overlooked. First, to Mary Ann Mann, who typed the manuscript and had complete faith in the book, our thanks.

Second, we would like to thank Robert L. Russel, District Attorney of the Fourth Judicial District of Colorado since 1964, who placed us in positions allowing for the development of knowledge which went into this work.

Foreword

The best deterrent to fraud and to the avoidance of financial loss due to fraud is an educated public. Only a well-educated consumer will have the knowledge and "healthy skepticism" necessary to spot a fraud before the financial loss occurs.

It is in the spirit of public education that this book was written. The authors are prosecutors who specialize in the investigation and prosecution of fraudulent schemes and who well understand the limitations of the criminal justice system in protecting the public from financial losses due to those schemes. The hope is that sharing our knowledge and experience regarding fraudulent schemes will serve to make the reader more alert and more able to identify a scheme before he pays money to its perpetrator. To accomplish this, the book is organized in such a way as to cover a wide variety of schemes, which are categorized, as far as possible, to facilitate identification by subject matter.

Undoubtedly there are books that examine particular schemes in a more comprehensive manner than this one, and certainly there are fraudulent schemes that are not covered in this book. The intent of the authors is to cover the vast majority of the most prevalent schemes to an extent that would be of assistance to the reader in understanding and identifying essential elements of particular frauds. Ironically, the test of our success is the extent to which the reader feels that the book was a good investment of time and money.

FRAUD & DECEiT: HOW TO STOP BEING RIPPED OFF

1

Business Opportunity and Investment Frauds (The Deal of a Lifetime)

COMMODITY FUTURES FRAUD

Lured by the promise of substantial returns that will keep them ahead of the inflation rate, well-heeled Americans are turning to the commodity futures market in large numbers. The influx of rank amateurs into a game best reserved for professionals has made it an attractive arena for the unscrupulous to perpetrate a variety of fraudulent schemes.

For the uninitiated, the term "commodity" encompasses all goods and articles and all services, rights and interests for which there is a market for contracts for future delivery of the goods or service. The most actively traded commodities include precious metals, grains, livestock and government financial paper. A futures contract is an agreement to buy or sell (i.e., to take or make delivery of) a stated amount of the commodity at some future date and at an agreed upon price. Thus, a futures contract is (hopefully) an educated guess about the state of supply and demand and hence about what the price of a commodity will be in future months. Contracts are traded, in standardized quantities, by delivery months.

Suppose you buy a November soybean contract on April 1. You're agreeing to accept delivery and pay for 5,000 bushels of soybeans when the contract expires in November. The cost was $7.07 per bushel or a total of approximately $35,000.00. You actually only pay $1,500.00 which is the minimum required under the regulations of, for example, the Chicago Board of Trade. If the price of soybeans moves up, you have a paper profit and can actualize the profit by selling the contract at a chosen time. In any event you're likely to sell before November because you don't really want 5,000 bushels of soybeans. In fact it is unusual to take delivery on a contract except perhaps when precious metals are involved. The bad news comes when the market moves down, because you must come up with additional margin, or sell at a loss.

The most blatant commodities fraud is a classic boiler room operation in which fly-by-night organizations, with fancy names, telephone affluent persons and subject them to a highly sophisticated and subtly high pressure pitch. The makeshift operation involves a battery of telephone salesmen set up at a prestigious address. The investor's money is wired to the caller's bank account and in a matter of two weeks to a month the entire operation is closed up and moves on.

Legitimate commodities brokers also solicit over the phone and ask for substantial funds to open accounts, so it is necessary to be well informed in order to spot the boiler room operation. In almost every instance, the boiler room operator will be promoting a commodity that is currently in vogue, whether it is gold, crude oil or whatever. He'll be playing on the average person's limited grasp of current events as well as what that person thinks will be hot items in the future. He'll also virtually guarantee large profits, a fraud in itself. The initial telephone pitch may be followed up by promotional literature and then a second phone call, all in quick succession. There's a demand for quick action and a request to wire necessary funds. A check is unacceptable to the boiler room operator because of the delays in payment it entails.

The boiler room operator's product may be called many things, but it is definitely not a futures contract. What they usually claim to be peddling is a "deferred delivery" contract which is in essence an option on commodities. But such a contract does not exist in U. S. markets anymore, having been banned in 1978.

If your investment in a bogus operation pays any sort of return it's likely a form of bucket shop operation where funds extracted from one customer are used to pay "profits" to another as a method of setting him up for a bigger kill.

Even if you manage to avoid the boiler room operator there are pitfalls in the legitimate futures market. A dishonest broker might intentionally fail to execute your order. If the price of the commodity goes down he assesses your account for the "loss" and pockets that amount. If the price goes up he informs you that a clerical error caused your order not to be executed. Watch the monthly statements closely, as well as the confirmations that should accompany each transaction.

If a commodities investor finds that 40 to 50 percent of his equity is disappearing into brokerage commissions he is almost certainly the victim of "churning" by his broker. Churning is a practice of excessively turning over an account in order to generate commissions. If you suspect your broker of churning, find a new one.

The most sophisticated kind of commodities fraud is manipulation of underlying commodities futures prices or entire contract markets. This generally requires cooperation between brokers and commodities traders utilizing complex techniques of manipulation over long periods of time.

Given the complexity and public misunderstanding of commodities trading, the potential for fraud is almost infinite. And it's always the amateur that falls prey to the scams. If you want to deal in commodities, learn as much as you possibly can. Your investment sophistication is your best protection against fraud.

If at any point you suspect fraud in commodities dealing you should contact the Commodity Futures Trading Commission, the federal agency that regulates the futures business. It is the task of the Commodity Futures Trading Commission to assure that markets operate fairly and competitively, free from manipulation. Part of the regulatory scheme includes registration of all persons and firms who buy or sell futures contracts. Registration requirements assure that the firm or salesman has met minimum financial requirements. Moreover, anyone opening a commodity futures account is entitled to a risk disclosure statement detailing the risks involved. (*See also* the section on Securities Fraud.)

FRANCHISING AND VENDING-MACHINE FRAUDS

Purchase exclusive territory!

Minimum investment secured by inventory. Are you tired of the 9-to-5 drag? Do you want to be your own boss? Set your own hours? Determine how much money you want to make? If so this opportunity for growth is for you.

It could almost be a form advertisement. Fill in the blanks with the name of the product, company or service and you have *the* chance of a lifetime.

Franchises can, in fact, offer tremendous opportunities and it is certainly true that many persons have become wealthy this way. Some of the most visible successes are the fast food industry franchises that now blanket the nation. But for every person who has made money through a franchise opportunity, there are at least ten times that many who have lost every cent they invested.

The message to prospective franchise purchasers is that they should carefully investigate all aspects of the opportunity before investing. You should always have qualified professionals, including your attorney and C.P.A., examine the legal and financial aspects of the franchise agreement.

Some other considerations include how long the franchising company has been in existence, its potential for growth and the experience and background of its management. Also one should require an audited statement of its assets and liabilities, preferably done by an independent auditor.

If the company appears to pass all of the above tests then consider the product or service. What is the acceptance of the product or service in other communities and will it meet the same success in your community? Is the product unique or are similar products or services offered from other sources which are more competitive in price or quality? If the product or service is new in your community, who is going to pay for advertising and promotion? What restrictions does the franchising agreement impose on you or upon potential competitors buying another franchise from the company?

Naturally there are numerous other questions that should be asked and satisfactorily answered, but even if the company and the product appear desirable, is this an opportunity for you?

A complete analysis of your assets and liabilities should be superimposed over the factors concerning the business. How much time will you be able to devote to the enterprise? Do you have the expertise to be able to compete in this field? How do your assets stack up? Will you be able to handle operating expenses plus maintaining a reserve for the unexpected? What type of staff is required? Is this a business you can handle alone or does it require a large staff? If it requires a staff do you have the experience to train and supervise employees? And, can you afford the outlay of capital required to enter the field? Remember, no one will run your business as well as you will. If you cannot do it, someone else won't.

Legitimate franchisors are also interested in the answers to all of the above questions, as their growth is dependent upon the success of the franchisees. That is true unless the franchisor is merely setting up a modified pyramid. If he is more interested in establishing a distribution system than in selling the product or services to the consumer, *beware!*

A necessary prerequisite for you, before even proceeding to all of the above questions, is to ask for the names, addresses and telephone numbers of all other franchise holders. Check with them. Ask the distributor to arrange for interviews. If he won't provide that basic comparative information, look elsewhere.

Generally, companies that require large initial payments and provide you with small amounts of information should be avoided.

These very same rules apply to would-be sellers of vending machines, video games and other rack products. The sellers frequently guarantee fantastic locations, machines that require little or no servicing and competitive prices.

These opportunities are frequently advertised in newspapers or other periodicals as a means for the small investor to get a start. Machines may sell for as little as $695.00, with a promise that with the investment of just a few hours a week the machine will rapidly pay for itself and begin making money.

The salesman promises you high-traffic locations that will yield tremendous results and tells you the company will obtain the location for you and place the machine.

After you invest, several things may happen. First, the salesman may never again grace your door and the out-of-state supplier may not even provide you with a machine. Second, if you do receive the machine it may have a retail value of one-tenth what you paid for it. After placement, you find that it continually malfunctions and that parts to repair it are unavailable. Third, you may find that the high-traffic location promised you is in a service station next to another machine that sells the same product for less. Warranties and guarantees are not honored and supplies are difficult to obtain as well as being so expensive that you cannot resell at a profit.

One of the variations is to sell a machine to a person at a relatively cheap price contingent upon an exclusive purchasing arrangement for the vended products. Thus you are tied to the supplier for two years and his prices are substantially higher than those of the regular wholesale market.

There's also the problem of the company making unwarranted claims about the product. When you attempt to sell it using the same information, you find yourself in a position of being unable to merchandise the product without making illegal claims to customers.

Almost invariably you find that the servicing and stocking of machines takes more time than estimated, especially when the locations are poor and spread out around the city. When you divide earnings into hours you find yourself working for less than $1.00 per hour — not a very good return on time, let alone investment.

In vending machines and franchising, as in all business endeavors, there is risk. By being careful and thoroughly investigating you will not eliminate risk, but you will eliminate unnecessary risk.

INVENTION MARKETING FRAUDS

Just imagine inventing a product that would replace the safety pin. It could mean a fortune to you.

Every inventor has a dream of creating and profiting from that creation. But few are equipped to bridge the gap between invention and production and to then take the quantum leap into marketing. They seek assistance that is legitimately available from many sources including patent attorneys and marketing, research, development and business consultants. For the unwary there is yet another choice. They have an idea. And they respond to an advertisement that promises to turn ideas into inventions and inventions into profits. The firm first will research the field to see if someone else has beaten you to the punch. It will then design the product, take care of obtaining patents and even help you with production and marketing. Armed with your idea, the firm does basic research and finds the idea unique. A report written in glowing terms comes to you. It promises huge returns at minimal investment. So you pay the $1,000.00 necessary to proceed. The company writes and tells you it has obtained a patent. It tells you a market is ready to be tapped and all you need do is invest $5,000.00 more. Shortly thereafter a prototype is developed. Production is ready to begin if you can obtain the necessary financing. You later find, much to your chagrin, that there was no patent obtained and that, in fact, one could not have been obtained. You also learn that the company was going through the same routine with four other persons, all of whom had submitted the identical idea. Net loss is $9,500.00 multiplied by four other persons. Net gain to the fraudulent company in return for no legitimate service is $38,000.00. And you could have saved all that money by a careful selection of a company to assist you.

Don't just respond to the ad. Check on the firm and its officers. What qualifications do they have to perform promised services? How long has the firm been in business? Obtain a list of satisfied customers and also check to see if any products have ever been taken from idea stage through marketing. And *don't* take the salesman's word for it. If the company is legitimate it will be happy to provide sufficient information to allow you to verify its claims.

Your replacement for the safety pin can perhaps make a fortune for phony consultants while making nothing for you.

LAND FRAUD

There is a deep need that seems to compel thousands of urban dwellers to "return to the sod" even if the sod consists of a waterless 5-acre tract in the middle of the Arizona desert. This fact, combined with the erroneous presumption that land is always a good investment, has allowed unscrupulous promoters to make literally billions of dollars from land fraud.

There are many variations to land fraud. Two basics are the resale of cheap land at inflated prices and the "new city" concept. A third variety is the Tennessee land fraud.

Take the first concept. To perpetrate this fraud one needs large quantities of cheap land, little or no governmental regulation, minimal legal work and a tremendous advertising and sales program. A huge ranch is ideal, especially if it has been a marginal producer and has paper water rights that will take years to litigate. Developers can tell investors there is plenty of water available while neglecting to explain the nature of the water rights and the fact that in the long run this type of water right is so far down the line of priorities that it will result in absolutely no water ever flowing into the old ranch boundaries.

The promoters pick up the land for something like $100.00 an acre. If possible, they put it on a long-term contract so that the initial investment is minimal. The land is then surveyed and the 10,000 acres replatted into 1- to 10-acre tracts. Next, colorful brochures are printed showing the tremendous view and delighting the reader with wonderful promises of tremendous profits to be made through the purchase of this "virgin land." And of course the land is sold on a contract-for-sale basis meaning you get title when you completely pay off the note. Naturally the promoters will be happy to carry the note at a "reasonable" rate of interest.

Thousands of persons purchase by mail land that they have never set foot upon. Two years later, while on vacation, they decide to drive down and see their property. They finally find the ranch and travel several cow trails trying to determine which lot belongs to them. They're not quite sure they ever found the right one. Upon returning home they reevaluate the investment and decide to sell. But there is no market and the developer will not list the property. He still has unsold property from the initial ranch purchase. So the purchaser stops making payments. The promoter merely cancels the contract, keeps all monies paid, and resells the land to someone else.

It's a great deal for the promoter. Figure 10,000 acres at $100.00 per acre equals an investment of $1 million. If he buys the land at 10 percent down he puts up $100,000.00. Add another $100,000.00 for expenses to resell. Now figure 1-acre tracts at $1,000.00 and 10-acre tracts at $10,000.00 (to make the mathematics easy). If our promoter sells 1,000 acres he has made $1 million. He now has $800,000.00 cash and a twenty-year mortgage with a balance owing of $900,000.00. He makes payments for two years during which time he reduces the mortgage to $800,000.00 leaving $700,000.00 cash left out of the initial sales. Assume he sells 4,000 more acres for a gross return of $4 million. If he has spent the $700,000.00 over this time period that leaves only the $4 million. Now, still owing $800,000.00 for the land, he declares bankruptcy, leaving the investors and the seller of the ranch holding the bag.

You can be sure he can show debts far exceeding the value of the land and you can be equally sure he has managed to walk out of the deal with at least $2 million cash plus a living wage of $100,000.00 a year for the last two years' work. He departs leaving a jumble of legal problems concerning land ownership and unpaid mortgages, only to reappear in another state and start over, in another land scam.

If that doesn't appeal to you, how about a planned city? Many of the variables are the same, except that planned cities are usually created by subsidiaries of highly respected corporations.

One major distinction is that the type of subdivision is quite different and the price charged investors is substantially higher. After all, you are purchasing land in a future city and you are paying for the zoning. Residential lots may run from $3,000.00 to $5,000.00, multifamily lots from $10,000.00 to $25,000.00. And planned unit developments and commercial zoning can support price tags of up to $25,000.00.

In this scenario the company plots the entire development, or at least a large portion of it. Streets are laid out with "major thoroughfares" paved. Water is available (although seldom as much as the salesman promises) and water and sewer lines are installed. A beautiful club is built alongside a small man-made lake. Half a dozen businesses are started, along with some houses. Later an industry (subsidized by the developer) moves into the area. There is always a company controlled publication mailed to investors and it extols the virtues of the burgeoning young community.

The sales contracts are again contracts for sale. But if you really want to throw a monkey wrench into the works (assuming that you purchase property), take the contract to the county clerk and recorder and have it recorded. That shows that you have a legal interest in the land thus clouding title to it, which means the seller has to foreclose or try to buy you out if you decide to quit making payments. He cannot merely keep your money, tear up your contract and resell the land. He will not like this, as foreclosure is not free. He may decide it is cheaper to return a portion of the monies you have paid.

A Tennessee land fraud works only on investors not familiar with the history of land grants in Tennessee and western North Carolina. Local residents are aware of who owns what in the area — and they know that registered deeds do not insure land ownership. Virtually anyone, for a $5.00 investment, can obtain title to thousands of acres of land. And if a prospective purchaser bothers to check to see if the deed is registered in the county land records, he will find that it is. The careless investor, satisfied with the legal description in the deed, makes his investment. And the seller takes his tremendous profits and disappears. The purchaser has just taken title to the Brooklyn Bridge.

The problem is that the deed is based on land grants issued 250 years ago and last surveyed when Andrew Jackson was president. Since then all surveyors' landmarks have disappeared. Under the Homestead Acts of the 1860's, homesteaders earned title to those lands last surveyed in Andrew Jackson's time. It is the surveys of *1832*, however, that are the basis for the deed that the fraudulent sale is based upon. Since homesteaders have earned clear title to the land

and these titles have then been passed down to subsequent purchasers, these rights are legally considered superior to those based upon land grants, meaning the purchaser has paid thousands of dollars for an impressive-looking piece of paper signifying nothing.

Some of the land has been registered twenty-five to thirty times and presumably sold as many times, with each purchaser eventually finding his piece of paper to be worthless. It's analogous to using a quit claim deed, which states that if the seller has any interest in the land, he transfers that interest, whatever that may be, to the buyer.

Quit claim deeds are valuable under some circumstances, which is more than can be said for Tennessee land grant deeds that have actual value only to the seller.

There are legitimate land sellers. And there are numerous ways to help you choose the right ones.

1. Check with long-time real estate salespersons in the area. What do they think of the investment?
2. Would they list the property for sale?
3. What is the reputation of the seller? How long has he been in business?
4. What is the price compared to other comparable land?
5. Was the land recently sold to the subdivider?

In addition, be sure to have an attorney check all contracts *before* you sign them. And have a qualified financial advisor assess the value of the land. Don't buy land sight unseen!

Remember never to fall for high-pressure tactics. If the deal was that good, the seller wouldn't have it on the market and the salesman would have either purchased it himself or offered it to a friend long before you arrived. Free knives, gasoline, hot dogs or other prizes are nice bonuses but they generally precede purchase of overinflated land.

When considering such a purchase scrutinize it as carefully as you would a lot or house in your community. If it cannot at least compare with the value of a lot in your hometown it's probably not the greatest deal of a lifetime — except for the seller.

PONZI SCHEMES

The basic idea has been in use for centuries but the modern version of the Ponzi bears the name of the man who perpetrated a multimillion dollar fraud in turn-of-the-century New England.

Charles Ponzi dealt in promises of untold riches based on international postage markets. He sold investors on the fact that by trading stamps between various nations they could, in fact, make profits ranging from 10 to 200 percent. His situation was unique because at that time such profits could actually have been made, had there been a way to exchange the stamps.

Ponzi invested the equivalent of perhaps $2.00 to investigate whether the idea worked in theory. He had friends or relatives in other countries buy stamps, which he exchanged elsewhere. With that knowledge safely in hand, Ponzi was prepared to offer investors tremendous returns in very short periods of time. No one, until much much later in the scheme, checked to see if large quantities of stamps were being exchanged or even if there was a way around the multitudinous governmental restrictions.

Ponzi's scheme is simple to understand. It is merely a mathematical progression and a variation of a pyramid promotion. Money taken from second-level investors is used to pay back initial investors and to satisfy the promised high rates of return on investment.

It appears that tremendous amounts would be required but Ponzi soon discovered that most investors left the initial investment in his company and many even re-invested their interest earnings. Thus he was able to siphon off large sums much earlier than anticipated.

The Ponzi scheme works perfectly so long as there is a continuous flow of new investors. When the source of new money dries, the entire house of cards collapses.

This continual promotion and growth is necessary. Any successful Ponzi scheme has elements of a pyramid promotional scheme. Therein lies the problem, as exemplified in the simple chart below. Assume that you invest in the Ponzi scheme at level 256. In order for you to realize a return along with your 255 companions at least another 256 investors must be recruited.

$$256$$
$$512$$
$$1024$$
$$2048$$
$$4096$$
$$8192$$
$$16384$$

Each doubling requires more and more recruits until at the twenty-ninth level something like 268,435,456 participants must be enrolled — more than the entire population of the United States. Shortly thereafter more people theoretically are participating than presently inhabit the earth.

What everyone fails to realize is that a Ponzi or a pyramid is really only a means of redistributing money rather than of accumulating new capital from investment. But that doesn't stop the hucksters. They are after your money and your loss is not their concern. They are aware that some Ponzi schemes have lasted for six to eight years before disintegrating.

That is easily understood when one examines the psychology of a Ponzi scheme. As an example, suppose that a friend of yours tells you that he recently invested $10,000.00 in Overseas Oil Company Ltd. Six weeks after he invested he received a dividend of $5,000.00 on his investment. Three months after that he received another $7,500.00 payment and he still has his initial $10,000.00 invested in the company. You thoroughly trust your friend and the excellent return reinforces your estimate of the situation. So you invest. Six weeks later you receive an initial return of $2,500.00 and you tell everyone you know about the opportunity; they in turn invest.

Your returns are slow and it takes a long time (sometimes forever) to get your initial investment back. But with the word of this investment spreading like wildfire the money flows in from everywhere. No one bothers to check and see that the money is not being used for any investment at all, but is merely being recirculated with the promoter raking off large chunks for expenses and for his own return on investment, which was usually minimal.

If an investor or governmental agency probes deeply enough into a Ponzi scheme, it can normally be shown to have minimal or nonexistent legitimate assets. Further, the mathematics usually will not stand a close scrutiny.

An example of a Ponzi-type scheme was the Oklahoma corporation that sold interests in its oil drilling operations to many very well-known persons, including Hollywood stars and Wall Street financial wizards. The money was never invested as represented. But large returns to initial investors taken from subsequent investors got the snowball rolling. By the time the scheme was uncovered it was a multimillion dollar rip-off.

There is probably no sure way to recognize a Ponzi. It can take nearly any shape. But a good tip is the promise of huge returns in short time periods with no risk attached. One of the cardinal rules of investment is that the safer an investment is, the lower return it usually pays. High returns go with high-risk projects which stand a very high chance of failure.

Another tip-off often is that even though the investment probably qualifies as a security, it is not registered with either the state or federal government.

Ponzi promoters try to maintain a level of professionalism consistent with the state of the financial community.

A recent example includes investment in a firm that pays returns with checks drawn on very small banks in out-of-the-way places. When someone pushes the promoters for a return they receive certificates of deposit drawn on offshore banks in Anguilla. When these are presented to the offshore bank they are either not claimed at the post office or are not honored.

Eventually the investor is dumped and may contact a law enforcement agency, which then attempts to follow a very cold trail to the source.

Ponzi was unique in that area. He was highly visible to the very end, and when his paper empire collapsed, several banks that had become embroiled in his financial structure also fell.

Regardless of the structure of the Ponzi scheme, the ultimate result is the same. You lose!

PYRAMID PROMOTIONAL SCHEMES

A pyramid scheme, in its most unsophisticated form, is better known as a "chain letter." The essence of the scheme is that there is no product or service being sold. Profits are derived through the continued recruitment of persons into the chain. Each new member pays a certain sum, which goes to those above him in the chain, and then sets out to recruit others so that he may similarly reap a profit. The term pyramid is descriptive because all such schemes take a pyramid shape when charted. And therein lies the rub. Such schemes cannot escape falling prey to the cruel realities inherent in the laws of probability.

The absence of a product insures that whatever profit made by those at the top of the pyramid will come out of the pockets of those at the bottom of the chain. In fact, probability studies of pyramid schemes show that if a pyramid progresses to any extent, less than 10 percent of the participants (at the very top of the pyramid) can expect any significant return on their investment and at least one-half of the participants will lose their entire investment.

Pyramid schemes that request the mailing of money or other items of value are generally in violation of postal regulations. If no money or item of value is involved a chain letter is not in violation of postal laws, unless it contains threats of violence to the recipient.

Many pyramid schemes that are rampant today are merely chain letters with semisophisticated trappings. Whether they go by the name of Businessman's Club, Circle of Gold, or whatever, the recruitment of persons is still the object and the mathematical realities remain the same. A chain letter by any other name is still a chain letter.

Unfortunately, the past twenty years have also seen the proliferation of complex pyramid sales schemes. Two such schemes that have been most prominent are the multilevel distributorship and the founder-membership plan. The typical multilevel distributorship plan involves the promotion of a line of products in an apparent franchise-type arrangement. The plans generally include several levels of distributorships and individuals buy into the distributorship at a particular level by paying the company an initial fee based on the level of entry. Thereafter the individual earns "commissions" by selling the company's products to the public and to those at lower levels in the distribution chain. Since the distributor profits by being a link in the product distribution chain the primary emphasis of the entire organization is on recruiting more investor-distributors rather than on retailing products. Recruitment to such multilevel schemes is typified by meetings or parties with high-pressure salesmanship and false enthusiasm by professional promoters who create the expectation of overwhelming financial returns from minimal time and effort. Multilevel sales schemes have typically involved such products as fuel additives, cosmetics, vitamins, fire and burglar alarms, clothes, soap products, household items and self-motivation courses.

The founder-membership plan involves an investor becoming a founder-member by buying an expensive product, generally at several times its retail value. The combined investment of the founder-members provides capital for the formation of a business that will be owned and operated by the promoters. Each founder is given the opportunity to recruit other founders, who join by paying an inflated price for the product. Once a member, the founder distributes buyer cards to potential customers of the business or provides names of potential customers to the promoters. When the business begins operation the founder-member receives a commission for each sale to a buyer he recruited. Thus participants are lured by the promise of earning profits even before the business begins, by recruiting other founder-members and by the prospect of future profits from sales after the store opens.

Each of these schemes is characterized by substantial investments by participants and quick profits for a small group of promoter-organizers. After obtaining initial investment money, the promoters typically show little desire to actually operate an effective product sales scheme. These schemes suffer from the fact that there is a limited number of potential recruits and as such they have the inherent instability of a chain letter. The system of recruitment will eventually collapse. As a result the promoters of all pyramid schemes must become adept at blinding potential recruits to the realities of the scheme. However, it is difficult to cover up one highly discernible telltale sign of pyramid schemes: The emphasis is placed on the recruitment of other individuals as a way to achieve large profits.

It was not until the late 1960's and early 1970's that the potential for pyramid sales schemes became truly apparent. That period saw the rise and fall of the pyramid empires of Glenn W. Turner (Koscot Interplanetary, Inc., Dare To Be Great, and Glenn W. Turner Enterprises). Thousands of people lost hundreds of thousands of dollars attempting to rise above mediocrity by daring to be great, and for the first time lawmakers learned of the ominous financial ramifications of pyramid schemes. States began to pass legislation dealing with pyramid sales and referral or multilevel sales plans. Typically these statutes define a pyramid scheme as a program in which a person gives valuable consideration for the chance to receive compensation by finding new participants for the program. The majority of state laws contain blanket prohibitions of pyramid schemes while others are regulatory in nature. In addition, the Federal Trade Commission has had success attacking such schemes as an unfair or deceptive act or practice in commerce. But perhaps the most creative and most effective approach to combating the financial losses inherent in pyramid schemes has been the utilization of state and federal securities laws. Courts on both the federal and state levels have declared that an investment in a pyramid scheme constitutes the offer and sale of a security, thereby subjecting the investments to registration requirements. Registration requires full disclosure regarding the investment. It was securities prosecutions that led to the eventual demise of Glenn Turner's various pyramid schemes. Such schemes have traditionally preyed on the uninformed, and when the uninformed become informed through full disclosure, they will rarely invest.

RAISING CREATURES GREAT AND SMALL — FOR A PROFIT

Many city dwellers are fascinated by the prospect of raising animals for profit. Maybe it's a subconscious desire to return to a more rural lifestyle. Or maybe it is just because they like to have pets and are thrilled at the prospect of making money while raising pets. Sometimes it just looks like a good way to make a fast buck. The result is that many people are susceptible to the often exaggerated and sometimes downright deceitful sales pitch of someone trying to sell them on raising animals as a profitable business opportunity. Two examples that stand out, and are typical of the pitfalls present in all such schemes, are chinchilla raising and worm farming.

There are many professional chinchilla breeders who make good money. But there aren't nearly as many as salesmen would have you believe. The Federal Trade Commission estimates the public is bilked of $50 million each year by chinchilla ranch promoters using deceptive sales techniques. The sales pitch will incorrectly inform you that chinchilla raising takes very little time and can be easily accomplished in your home or garage. The salesman may also falsely claim that 4 to 6 offspring per female can be expected (1.5 to 2 is more accurate), and may exaggerate the market for chinchilla pelts. He may neglect to inform you that amateurs can expect a 20 percent death rate of newborn chinchillas per year and that disease can put you out of business in a hurry. Finally, the salesman may sell you low-quality animals for exorbitant prices. Any buy-back guarantee you receive is only as good as the company that offers the guarantee.

The problems with worm farming also stem from the misrepresentations of business opportunity promoters working on a commission basis. They can grossly overestimate the reproduction rate worm farmers can expect. Another false claim might involve the possible market for the product. One slick promoter falsified documents indicating there was a great market for worms in Asia as a protein supplement. Almost all fraudulent worm schemes have involved a promise that the promoter would purchase back all worms raised after a certain period of time so that the person raising the worms need not be concerned about marketing the product. The promise proves to be an empty one because the promoter is not around, or at least not in business, when the period of time expires.

Before you sign any contracts for business opportunities involving raising animals make the promoters substantiate any income projections. See the operations of other satisfied customers and make sure they're not just shills involved in the promotion scheme. Do some research of your own to evaluate reproduction claims and market conditions. Talk to those who successfully raise the animals in question to evaluate the feasibility of the business for you. Also contact consumer agencies to get information concerning the company involved or the general pitfalls involved in the business opportunity being promoted.

SECURITIES FRAUD

Starting with Kansas in 1911, almost all states have adopted some form of legislation to protect the public from fraudulent and deceptive practices in the offer and sale of securities. The vast majority of states have adopted, in whole or in part, the Uniform Securities Act, which parallels the federal securities legislation of 1933 and 1934. The combination of state and federal securities laws provides a very valuable tool to combat a wide range of investment frauds.

The basic question is whether a particular investment constitutes a security. In general, the securities laws have been liberally construed to encompass those situations where the investor expects that his profit will result primarily, if not entirely, from the efforts of those with whom he is investing. The more passive the investor's role in the investment, the more likely it is that a security is involved. This will encompass not only investments traditionally perceived as securities, such as stocks and bonds, but also investment contracts, limited partnerships and certain forms of franchise investment. The courts recognize investment contracts as any contractual investment in a common enterprise where the investor is led to expect profits from the efforts of others. The comprehensiveness of this concept is shown by the fact that the sale of a condominium has been held to constitute a security where the sale is accompanied by an agreement that rental rates, supporting services and promotion of the units will be controlled by a common agent. A significant development of relatively recent origin has been the inclusion of pyramid schemes or multilevel sales promotions in the definition of securities subject to regulation. In fact securities laws were largely responsible for the demise of the pyramid empire of Glenn W. Turner. (*See* the section on Pyramid Promotional Schemes.)

The essence of both federal and state securities regulations is the registration of securities offerings, the registration or licensing of persons dealing with securities and the prohibition of fraudulent acts in the offer or sale of securities. Registration requirements are designed to provide the potential investor with a full disclosure concerning the investment, including its potential risks, so that the investor may make a well-informed decision. As a result, the presumption is always in favor of the registration requirement and the issuer of securities generally bears the burden of showing that he qualifies for an exemption from registration. Both state and federal acts include exemptions from registration. Exemptions are generally permitted not because disclosure is unneccessary but because it is provided elsewhere, for example, through compliance with requirements for registration on a national stock exchange.

A private offering or private placement exemption is the one most commonly claimed by defendants who have not registered securities. The purpose of the exemption is to allow the sale of unregistered securities in situations where the investors, usually because of their limited numbers and preexisting relationship with the issuer of the securities, do not require the protection of the registration requirement.

While securities laws are extremely complex and largely incomprehensible to the average layman, there are some generalizations that potential investors should keep in mind. Pitfalls almost always arise when the security being sold is not listed on an exchange and the person selling the security is not a licensed broker with a licensed brokerage firm. If you are approached by someone to buy stock or otherwise make a "passive" investment in an enterprise and the person approaching you is not licensed and the investment is not listed on an exchange, extreme caution is appropriate. Generally speaking, if you do not have a preexisting personal or business affiliation with the person offering the stock and the business involved in the investment, then the security being offered will most likely have to be registered or qualified for an exemption on the basis of compliance with federal or state laws. In such cases you should insist on your right to a full disclosure contained in a registration statement or prospectus. If a person sells unregistered securities that should be registered and is not licensed to do so, a variety of criminal offenses are being committed. Further, the antifraud provisions of the securities laws, which prohibit misleading representations in the offer and sale of securities and any course of business that acts as a deceit on the stockholders, apply whether or not the stock is registered.

Your state's securities commission is available to let you know if a particular security is registered and to better inform you concerning the intricacies of the applicable securities laws. Do not invest until you are convinced that the investment is in compliance with the law.

It should not be assumed that if you deal with registered stock and licensed brokers, you are immune from securities fraud. Some securities theft rings operate on a large and complex scale. Their schemes may involve the utilization of cooperative "inside" people who substitute worthless securities for valuable ones and manipulate records to deceive the auditors. Or a brokerage house employee may give a fictitious customer's name to the transfer agent of stock that is to be "delivered out," thereby diverting securities into the hands of thieves.

Another common scheme involves a customer who has received a stock certificate and then claims that he has not received it. He goes through the procedure to obtain a replacement certificate and uses the duplicate certificate to pledge as collateral on a loan.

Securities fraud has an international flavor as some complex schemes are known to involve a loosely organized syndicate comprised of con men from several different countries. Further, many frauds are more readily perpetrated outside the jurisdiction of the Securities and Exchange Commission. Organized crime elements not only commit many securities frauds but also facilitate frauds by others by operating a fencing network for stolen securities.

Warning signals for securities fraud include:

1. Securities are offered at private sale at a substantial discount from currently quoted prices.
2. The proper number of shares is accounted for by an inventory check but the number of certificates on hand does not correspond with records.
3. A proposed securities transaction involves secretive foreign elements.
4. The assets of an unfamiliar firm are principally composed of obscure securities.
5. Offshore financial institutions are involved in the securities transaction.
6. Undue delay by a broker in "delivering out" a requested security.

Fraudulent stock certificates are often characterized by one-color printing, the absence of a human figure, the lack of a three-dimensional look and overall unprofessional appearance.

A form of securities fraud that leaves the average consumer with little in the way of self-defense is stock manipulation by insiders. Perhaps all that can be said is that there is comprehensive and effective federal legislation in the area of inside information, conflicts of interest and self-dealing. Those who have a reasonable suspicion that such manipulation is occurring should contact the regional office of the Securities and Exchange Commission.

As a final comment, in the area of securities fraud, as in most of the matters treated in this book, the application of healthy cynicism is perhaps the best investment a consumer can make. (*See also* the section on Commodity Futures Fraud.)

WORK-AT-HOME SCHEMES

Few opportunities sound more attractive to a person or family struggling financially than the chance to make a large amount of money by working in their own home in their spare time. Because of this fact, thousands of Americans pay 25¢ to $25.00 for information about work-at-home jobs that either do not exist or are virtually worthless. Housewives in particular, who want to supplement the family income, are easy prey for the dishonest promoter of work-at-home schemes. The fact is that finding a worthwhile work-at-home opportunity in the want ads is not easy to do. Sadly, some schemes continue to reap profits much longer than necessary because victims tend not to complain about such small losses in order to avoid the embarrassment and the "hassle."

The most typical work-at-home scams will involve a newspaper ad that might read "Earn $100.00 per week at home in your spare time addressing envelopes." The reader immediately envisions himself addressing envelopes for some large corporate enterprise while he's watching his favorite TV shows. What could be easier? Upon his initial inquiry he is asked to send $10.00 for the details of the opportunity. When he sends in the money he receives a "kit" that tells him how to place an ad in the newspaper identical to the one he responded to and sucker other people into paying him $10.00 in the same manner he was suckered into paying $10.00. In other words, the only addressing envelopes that is done is in response to inquiries from the new crop of suckers.

Another common fraudulent work-at-home scheme might begin with the placing of an ad that claims you can "earn up to $4.00 per hour sewing baby shoes in your own home." Those inquiring are required to pay a small registration fee and demonstrate their sewing skill by sewing a pair of baby shoes. The essence of the scheme is that every one of the prospects fails to measure up to the promoter's "standards." As a result, without ever making a single product, the promoter pockets thousands of dollars in fees, plus lots of baby shoes.

Other work-at-home scams involve the paying of a franchise fee for the right to sell products from your home. Once the promoter has your franchise fee either the product is not forthcoming or the product proves extremely unmarketable, contrary to the promises of the promoter.

Telephone solicitation work is another appealing scam. It is wise for the potential work-at-home telephone solicitor to insist on answers to certain questions about the product to be sold and the company involved. If satisfactory answers are not forthcoming, he should look elsewhere. Many solicitors have worked hard to raise lots of money for what turned out to be a bogus operation and have been left high and dry with a check that bounced to show for their efforts.

Other suspect home-bound opportunities might involve mailing circulars, clipping newspaper articles, making jewelry or painting novelty items.

Unfortunately, not all work-at-home business opportunity frauds take a "nickle and dime" approach. Life savings may be involved. One such case involved a Las Vegas corporation that advertised in newspapers nationwide. It claimed it would contract with individuals as manufacturers of certain custom auto parts. The parts would be manufactured at the investor's home and sold to the corporation, which would make its profit by marketing the parts. An income of $2,000.00 per month, working part-time, was projected. A lump-sum payment of $8,000.00 gave the investor a plane ticket to Florida for a two-day training session. At its conclusion he was given a document indicating he was a certified manufacturer for the corporation. He was told that the necessary materials to begin his business would be delivered within 30 days. He returned home and spent another $1,500.00 fixing up his garage as a suitable work area. When nothing was delivered within 30 days he called the company to complain. Eventually, over the next few months, a few materials arrived but never the right combination of materials necessary to manufacture a part. After several more months of complaining he finally received materials sufficient to produce one part. When he sent the part to the corporation in Las Vegas, it was returned by the corporation as not meeting specifications, something the investor was told would never happen.

Fraud would be difficult to prove on the basis of this single incident. But it was eventually discovered that there were no less than 400 victims across the country who had the exact same story to tell. Each step of the scheme had been carefully calculated. It is a good example of the extent to which some schemes will go. It would have been easier to have just taken the money and run, but the planned scenario allows the scheme to work for a longer period of time. While the perpetrators may be successfully prosecuted, it is unlikely that the economic loss to the victims can ever be rectified.

Suspicion is the consumer's greatest virtue when he's considering potential work-at-home opportunities. Figures representing income potential should be backed up by statistics that show what percentage of previous investors have made that amount, and an independent means to verify the statistics should be provided. Always investigate fully before you invest, not after.

The business opportunity section of a newspaper is not the only, and is frequently not the best, source of work-at-home opportunities. Often, certain types of businesses in your community will be responsive to a request to contract for work done at home. The advantage of such situations lies in the fact that you know whom you're dealing with and you know they're in a business other than collecting money from you.

2

Merchandising Frauds (Things Aren't Always As They Appear To Be)

AUTO SALES FRAUD

Whether you're buying a new car or a used car you should be alert for certain deceptive practices that can cheat you of the bargain you think you're getting.

For the new car purchaser, the first precaution is to make sure the car you're buying is, in fact, new. Many persons have been told the car they were buying was new, have believed it was new and have paid a new car price, only to later find that the car has been previously titled to another individual. Other purchasers have unknowingly been sold demonstrator models that were represented as new cars. In most states it is now unlawful for a car dealer to sell a demonstrator model without specifically designating it as such. Chances are that an attempt to pass off a used car as a new car will also involve an illegal odometer rollback. If information comes to your attention that leads you to believe that the car you bought, which was represented as being a new car, is not in fact new, bring your suspicions to the attention of the local law enforcement agency, as well as the state agency that regulates new car dealers.

A separate section of this book is devoted to the practice of "bait and switch" advertising. Such tactics are all too commonplace in the merchandising of new cars. When you arrive at a car lot in response to an attractive advertisement, the salesman may disparage the car on sale as a "crummy stripped down model" and attempt to sell you a more expensive vehicle packed with extras. Don't let him.

The first thing to recognize about purchasing a used car is that once you buy the car, its problems are your problems. Without written warranties, all used cars are purchased "as is." If the car falls apart five minutes after you leave the lot, it's your tough luck. So any mechanical inspection of a car you're thinking about buying should take place before the purchase.

A used car purchaser should always have a trusted and competent mechanic thoroughly inspect the car he is considering buying. He should be alert for cosmetic cover-ups of damages and defects. He should make sure the apparently good tires aren't just regrooved bald ones and make sure the new engine parts aren't really old parts covered with silver spray paint.

The used car purchaser should always be alert for an odometer rollback. An apparent low-mileage "gem" may in fact be a high-mileage clunker. Warning signals of a rollback include apparent tampering in the dashboard, misaligned speedometer digits, perforations in the odometer, sticking digits, old inspection stickers revealing higher mileage and an overall condition of the vehicle that is inconsistent with the alleged mileage.

A used car purchaser should also be alert for the "phantom seller" — a person who does not actually own the car or have authority to sell it. It may be that a lending institution has the title to a car and a purchaser will be out of luck because of the seller's inability to satisfy his obligation to the lending institution. Don't consummate a sale until you know the other party actually owns the car and that the title is readily available. Finally, all representations you're relying on in the purchase of a car should be written into your contract.

BAIT AND SWITCH ADVERTISING

As the name suggests, bait and switch advertising is a merchandising scheme whereby a merchant "baits" the customer into his store with an extremely attractive but insincere offer to sell a product or service and then "switches" the customer to a product or service that involves a higher profit to himself. The scheme is as old as the concept of sales and rare is the person who has escaped falling victim to bait and switch tactics. However, many victims of bait and switch never have perceived that they were taken.

The "bait" almost always consists of an advertisement that offers a product or service at an attractive price and that draws the public into the store or causes the public to otherwise contact the advertiser and arrange for personal contact with a salesman. The "switch" is harder to identify. It generally consists of one or more of the following practices:

1. A refusal to show the product advertised.
2. Disparagement in any respect of the advertised product or the terms of sale.
3. Requiring tie-in sales or other undisclosed conditions to be met prior to selling the advertised product or service.
4. A refusal to take orders for the product advertised for delivery within a reasonable time.
5. Showing or demonstrating a defective product that is unusable or impracticable for the purposes set forth in the advertisement.
6. Accepting a deposit for the product and subsequently switching the purchase order to a higher priced item.
7. Failure to make delivery of the product within a reasonable time or to make a refund therefor.

These practices are accompanied by a referral by the salesman to a substitute for the advertised product that he touts because of its superior quality or availability. The switch can range from being very simple to very sophisticated.

Consider a typical scenario for bait and switch advertising. You read in the Sunday newspaper that a local major appliance store is going to have a sale on brand X portable color television sets. You know that the advertised offer is a good one because your neighbor has owned a set like the one advertised for over a year, he's very happy with it and he paid $40.00 more than the price advertised. The sale is to run for Monday and Tuesday only and you're at the store when it opens at 9:00 A.M. on Monday. When you ask to see the advertised product one of two things might happen. You might be informed by the salesman that the advertised product is sold out and then told about another television set, perhaps a little larger, which is only $60.00 more. Chances are you're now in a buying mood and don't want to waste a trip downtown. So you fall prey to the switch. Or the pitch may be a little more sophisticated. The salesman takes you over to view the advertised set but then takes you aside and states in a near whisper, "The boss would kill me if he heard me tell you this, but that set has some real problems." He then pulls a Xerox copy of a page from *Consumer Reports* from his pocket; it shows two black dots in the "repair record" column, meaning that the set has a "worse than average" repair record. (The original only had one black dot, indicating an "average" repair record.) The salesman then touts another TV set, which costs $50.00 more, as having a good repair record that will result in greater savings over the long run. Your tendency is to be impressed with the guy's honesty. He's putting his job on the line to keep you from buying a lousy TV set. In truth, of course, the boss would be proud of the salesman for his perfect execution of the bait and switch sales technique, which the boss taught him.

Bait and switch advertising is prevalent in the sale of a wide range of products including meat, appliances and new cars, and in the promotion of many services including automotive and appliance repair. Almost all states now have legislation that makes the practice either a crime or a violation of consumer protection legislation that authorizes the local prosecutor to seek injunctive relief. Such laws require that if an ad does not contain a specific limitation on quantity, the store must have a supply of the product on hand that is sufficient to meet reasonable expected public demand. The laws also prohibit any disparagement of the advertised product itself while allowing discouragement of the customer on the basis of the product's suitability for his needs (i.e., a Volkswagen is not suitable for a family of eight).

A consumer responding to an ad for an item on sale should be extremely suspicious of any attempted switch. If, on arriving at the store, the salesman tells you that the advertised product is not of high quality, that it's defective or that it's sold out, or makes similar statements that encourage you to choose an unadvertised product, you should take your business elsewhere.

CONTEST WINNERS

It's nearly irresistible. You receive a postcard in the mail telling you that Lady Luck has at long last smiled upon you. CONGRATULATIONS! You're a Winner. And all you have to do to collect your prize is to present your lucky number at the showroom. Or maybe just sit through a *brief* presentation given to you and your spouse.

One of the favorites is to award transistor radios — and generally you'll receive the radio on demand. After all, how much can a small radio cost when it has an effective range of one mile, line of sight? The people giving you the prize are after bigger game. They want your signature on a contract. Whether it's soap or sewing machines the one thing you can be absolutely sure of is that you won't be buying a bargain.

Contest winners are often "chosen" from mailing lists or lists of persons who entered the contest at a state fair booth. On a list containing 10,000 names, there may well be 10 first-place winners and 9,990 second-place winners.

The first-place prize usually is valuable but even here the seller is running little risk as he knows the chances of one of the prizes being claimed, let alone 10, is quite small. And he knows if he gets a

10-percent response on the mailing he may sell 10 percent of those persons. One hundred sales, at his prices, will more than cover overhead, thank you.

Further, the refined operators have you come to their place of business so the 72-hour "cooling off" period in which a contract may be canceled is inapplicable. Once you sign, he doesn't want you to slip away. And immediately he'll discount the contract to the finance company so he will not be the one left holding the bag if you default on your payments.

Take a smoke alarm system as an example. Here the prize you win may be $500.00 off the cost of a complete system, installed. That leaves a balance of $635.00 plus interest. You finance a total of $1,100.00 over 24 months making your payments just under $50.00 per month. It's all for a good cause, the protection of your family. What you learn later is that you could have purchased a better system for under $100.00 — one on which the warranty would be honored.

There are numerous other variations. You might win a free sewing machine (on condition you purchase a cabinet or a 10-year service agreement). You get the idea.

Some of these contests require your initial participation. You must solve a puzzle or write a limerick. And regardless of the answer, or the quality of your rhyme, you are a WINNER. But the only thing you have really won is the opportunity to be overcharged. The Flim Flam Man wins again. This is not to say that reputable businesses never conduct contests nor that you can't be a winner. But when the "prize" is tied to a purchase, you almost always lose.

It's not that difficult to separate the contests from the come-ons if you don't allow yourself to be pressured. After all, if you are truly a winner, it shouldn't cost you exorbitant prices to collect the prize.

DECEPTIVE PRICING

There is a vast difference between advertising bargain items discounted for sale and deceptive pricing practices. The latter category encompasses a multitude of sins but the basic idea is the use of a price structure that appears to indicate the customer is receiving a bargain when, in fact, he is not. It is usually accomplished by describing the item for sale in unfamiliar terms or by not disclosing essential qualifications.

Many products are normally sold in specific units of measure. As an example, nails are sold by the pound. An ad offering nails for a penny apiece may sound attractive but when converted to the normal price per pound may well be a very high price.

A favorite subject for nondisclosure of essential terms is meat. An offer to sell at $1.55 per pound (20 to 60 percent less than advertised at your supermarket) if bought in quantity may turn out to be two or three times the $1.55 price after the meat is trimmed of bones and fat.

Before signing on the dotted line, be sure the bargain is a bargain. Sales are a fertile ground for deceptive pricing. To dramatize a bargain some stores will arbitrarily assign "regular" prices to goods when they were never, in fact, sold at that price. The sale price may exceed the actual regular price. (*See* the section on Going Out of Business Sales.)

Deceptive pricing is usually accompanied by high-pressure sales and double talk. Salesmen evade direct questions about quantities, quality and pricing practices. This is an area where your suspicious side should be well developed. When the warning signs appear do *not* buy until you have completely investigated and compared the price with others available on the same unit basis.

An ounce of prevention is indeed worth a pound of cure in this area, as most merchants who deal in deception don't stick around to rectify complaints.

ENCYCLOPEDIAS

There are all types of reference works on the market and to hear the sales pitches you would have to conclude that without access to each and every one of them in *your* home, your child is doomed to a life of illiteracy.

Now the salesman is aware that schools and libraries have available all sorts of reference works, so he has to make the product appear more attractive. That's usually done by his giving you an encyclopedia, or even a full reference set of twenty volumes. Your only obligation is to assist his company's advertising promotion. You see, you have been selected at random to preview this new edition and the company will give it to you if you will agree to merely write a letter of recommendation and promise to use the set. (After all, it wouldn't look right should someone happen to look at your bookcase and see dust collecting on the outside of the volumes.)

Finally he gets to the point. There is just one other minor consideration. To qualify for this special prepublication offer you must agree to purchase the update service, to be published annually over the next decade. That only makes sense because of the rapidly changing technology in the world. It just wouldn't do to have your child using outdated materials.

Of course, when you take the time to investigate you find that the cost of the ten single volumes exceeds the fair market value of the entire set. And you find it's necessary to finance the entire amount in advance. Thus you suddenly end up with 36 months' worth of payments and a reference work that the children put to use at least twice during their schooling.

The only thing that is really puzzling about this approach is how so many encyclopedias are available prior to publication.

FREEZER PLANS

There are so many pitfalls in purchasing food and freezers in a combined package that it is difficult to know where to begin. These programs are sold door-to-door or they may be hawked at the merchant's place of business after he has enticed you into the store. To protect yourself from fraudulent plans it is essential that you be aware of the average retail price of food freezers and, further, that you be relatively familiar with the various cuts of meat and their comparative costs.

The con man is going to have the best deal in town. He will sell you $500.00 worth of meat for $225.00 if you will purchase a food freezer and sign up for a 6-month supply of meat. The freezer costs you $600.00 and the meat sells for $1.50 a pound (cheap!). The total cost to you, including 150 pounds of meat, comes to $1,075.00, which is then financed for 12 months at 18 percent per annum. You have now assumed a payment of about $100.00 per month for the next year — but your meat is bought and you have a freezer. Of course, upon checking you find that the freezer has an average retail price of about $300.00. And you find that the meat was sold "hanging weight" so by the time excess fat and bone is removed you end up with half the amount you planned upon, effectively increasing the price per pound 100 percent. Further, the meat turns out to be U.S.D.A. "Good," which is the lowest of the top three U.S.D.A. grades and normally sells for less than prime or choice cuts. Even so, you don't feel too awfully bad until your 6-month supply of meat is exhausted in 2 months, leaving you owing $1,000.00 and in addition having to buy meat for your family for the next 10 months.

You could complain to the seller but he has probably gone out of business; even if the business still exists he is going to ignore your complaint. Naturally the contract you signed protects the seller and obligates you to make payments. Legally the con man has done everything possible to protect himself at your expense. Here's some protection for the buyer.

1. Never buy before comparing. Do not give in to high-pressure tactics.
2. Be sure you understand all the terms of the deal including the cuts and weights of beef, the costs and the interest charges.
3. Check the seller's reputation.

There are numerous agencies that can be contacted for assistance. Make use of them and your beef buy can result in savings for your family.

THE FUNERAL INDUSTRY

If there is one time that we anticipate that our worries will be over, it is at the moment of death. But for others, usually relatives of the deceased, the death of someone they love propels them into a bewildering world. It is then that a consumer finds himself confronted with funeral arrangements and a multibillion dollar funeral industry fraught with peril for the unwary.

As with any major industry, there are abuses. Some are applicable only to sales of services and products at the time of death. Other abuses occur only in cases where a person has made careful arrangements for his funeral well beforehand; state regulations (or the lack thereof) play a predominant role in protecting a customer's investment and thereby his choices involving his funeral and the disposition of his body.

Unscrupulous funeral directors are familiar with the time pressures necessitating a quick decision and the natural inclination of a bereaved relative to rely upon someone else. A greedy funeral director plays on this fact and also upon the impact of bereavement and perhaps guilt associated with the death. He sells unnecessary products or services to the representative of the deceased or he may convince the purchaser that burial of his relative in a cheaper casket is really tacky. "After all, this is the last time you will ever have an opportunity to do something for Aunt Matilda," he purrs. And thus an expensive casket is purchased and sent to the crematory when a simple container would have served the same purpose.

In chronological order, a funeral director can first obtain a jump on the competition when he learns of a death. It is the legal right of survivors to choose the funeral home (if no will or some sort of prepaid plan has been left by the deceased). If the funeral director chooses to ignore this right, relatives may be informed of the death by him. And he is aware of the reluctance survivors feel about moving a body, as well as of the statistics that show that at the time of death it is rare for more than one funeral home to be contacted.

If the funeral director proceeds with embalming without direct authorization from the family, he has strengthened the symbiotic tie that he developed. There is now a debt owed to the funeral director and a natural allegiance to him. At this point, very few families insist upon transferring the body to another funeral home.

The funeral director has a customer. It is now time for the sales pitch. Seldom, if ever, does he employ high-pressure tactics. There is no need as the family representative is vulnerable and high-pressure tactics might even offend him. In the sales area, the first choice revolves around the type of funeral selected. A traditional funeral implies an open casket. And the funeral director has a wide selection on display ranging from the cheap model in the corner (which has smudges on the lining) to the ornate coffin that sparkles on a dais in the center of the room.

The traditional funeral is the odds-on favorite as far as the funeral director is concerned, as it involves the greatest potential for profit.

A partial list includes:

1. The funeral home's use for viewing the body.
2. The use of the funeral home for services.
3. Rental of additional vehicles for use by the family.
4. Sale of casket.
5. Possible tie-in sales of funeral plot, grave liner and grave marker.
6. Incidental services including placing notices of death in the newspapers and procurement of death certificates.

The greater potential for abuse lies in item 6. The funeral home may act as agent in obtaining third-party services. Examples might include obtaining flowers from a floral shop or in placing newspaper notices. Newspapers generally consider "vital statistics" a paid advertisement and charge for each insertion, whereas an obituary is placed at the newspaper's discretion but there is no charge for its insertion.

If the newspaper is furnished with the information it will prepare the obituary.

Many funeral homes bill customers under a general heading without breaking down costs to the individual items. As an example, the funeral home could be charging for its services in ordering flowers or in supplying obituary information to newspapers. It could charge a premium over the cost for vital statistics, thus giving it an incentive to have the vital statistics printed more times than necessary. Many may also sell funeral clothes for display of the body. And the customer has no idea why the bill is so large. These items are over and above the normal charges for embalming, preparing the body and conducting the funeral. All of these costs hit the customer when he is particularly vulnerable.

He has few choices as most persons do not compare prices prior to choosing a funeral home. And should someone attempt to do so, he would have to personally visit each funeral home as most do not give out price information over the telephone.

Since there is such a wide disparity in prices and services available, there is untold room for abuse. Costs for a basic funeral can differ by hundreds of dollars, depending upon what "extras" are ordered.

Assuming one chooses an alternate to the traditional funeral, costs can be cut substantially. But even here an unscrupulous funeral director can convince a grieving relative that it is necessary to purchase a coffin for viewing the body prior to cremation. What that may mean is that the expensive coffin is also cremated.

The funeral offers an opportunity for what might best be described as price gouging or sale of unnecessary products or services by the funeral home. However, this area of the industry, at least, does provide some sort of service. That is not always the case with preneed plans, which have developed in an attempt to exploit publicity regarding the high cost of dying. These plans made their initial appearance in the early 1950's and this aspect of the industry has grown steadily since that time.

The preneed plan involves the sale of funeral and cemetery merchandise and services in advance of death. You select and pay for the funeral, thus removing the burden from your survivors. Sale of the services and products is generally accomplished by a small army of telephone solicitors and door-to-door salesmen buttressed by a saturation advertising campaign. Very high pressure sales tactics are utilized and thousands of people, almost all elderly, will sign up to purchase the full package. The sales are usually accomplished by cemeteries or mausoleums because the traditional funeral industry has chosen to ignore this area.

There are several areas of abuse.

1. Salesmen may take deposits and even collect payments without turning them in to the company. Thus at death no plan exists even though it has been paid in advance.
2. The company selling the plan may go bankrupt years later with the same result. This is less likely than it once was because of state trust requirements.
3. The plan may be redeemable only at a particular funeral home so that if you move across the country the value is substantially lessened. This problem is solved by many plans that allow redemption for cash, but usually at a discount.
4. The sales force is almost universally compensated solely on a commission basis, thus giving an incentive to misrepresent the plan and its benefits.

But the major problem, both from the standpoint of the industry and the consumer, are the states' trust requirements. Basically the states require that up to 85 percent of the monies paid to preneed plans be placed in trust to insure that the services will in fact be available years later at the time of death. Industry proponents argue that this is unreasonable as 15 percent is not even enough to pay sales commissions. Thus preneed sellers continually look for ways around this requirement, creating a potential problem for the relatives of a deceased. They may find that the preneed plan, paid for long ago and believed to be available, is not, or at least is not available as originally contemplated.

State legislatures have placed the responsibility for monitoring these trust accounts with various agencies, such as the State Insurance Commissioner. Major problems may develop if the responsible agency does not properly monitor the investments that trust funds make. The trust funds can be siphoned into affiliated industries and when they declare bankruptcy the preneed trust funds go with them, leaving no money for providing services.

The funeral industry generates revenues of $6 billion to $8 billion a year. It affects people when they are least able to make rational choices. The consumer, if he is to deal effectively with the situation, must attempt to make major decisions in the same manner he would if he were contemplating a major purchase of another item.

1. Ask about prices and compare prices and services even if this entails visiting different funeral homes.
2. Insist on a breakdown of prices charged for various services.
3. Resist all high-pressure tactics, especially in the preneed area. Sign only when you are sure of costs and are satisfied you wish to make the purchase.
4. Report immediately any incidents that might constitute a crime.

Grief can be compounded later by choices made when you are under stress at the time a relative dies. The situation is never pleasant but it need not also create an undue financial burden to be borne for years to come.

GOING OUT OF BUSINESS SALES

If your community is an average one you've probably got a furniture store in town that has had a "going out of business" or "inventory liquidation" sale at least three times in the last year. In fact it seems that whenever it's not having a going out of business sale it's having a grand opening sale. The fact is that going out of business and inventory liquidation sales have become highly profitable merchandising gimmicks that can serve to consistently deceive bargain-hunting consumers. Even when the business is actually closing its doors for good, consumers may not be getting the bargains they are being led to expect.

Inventory liquidation sales have long been used as a means of baiting customers into the store. The store may be moving, changing its name, closing temporarily or suffering from some other trumped up tragedy that allegedly necessitates the sale. The desperation manifested in the advertising is not genuine. In many cities this sort of advertising deception has been effectively deterred by local laws that require business holding going out of business sales to procure a license, actually go out of business and stay out of business for a definite period of time.

Deceptive pricing frequently accompanies a going out of business sale. Constant price reductions are part of the attraction of such sales and are easily manipulated. A dress marked "Was $55.00. Now $35.00" will be changed to "Was $70.00. Now $35.00" if it doesn't sell on the first day. Only the alleged regular price will change, never the actual selling price.

If the store going out of business is part of a chain, a liquidation sale should be viewed with special skepticism. In one documented case a high-quality clothing store chain was closing one of its downtown stores for lack of business. It procured a license for a two-month going out of business sale and advertised that everything in the store would be sold at whatever price it took to sell it. What the public was not told is that for the three months prior to the going out of business sale a considerable inventory adjustment had taken place. The most desirable merchandise, approximately 70 percent of the entire inventory, was moved from that store to other stores in the chain. Slow-moving merchandise from the other stores was brought in to replace it. In fact a great deal of merchandise, of much lower quality than the store had traditionally carried, was purchased and brought into the store just for the going out of business sale. An extensive advertising campaign was waged and the public was erroneously led to believe that desirable high-quality merchandise was being sold at "rock-bottom" prices. In reality the thousands of people who flocked to the sale were paying prices that were anything but a bargain. Sadly, few of them were conscientious enough to shop around and discover the stark realities of the matter. Perhaps the most revealing aspect of the entire situation was the fact that the sale was being orchestrated by a marketing consulting firm that specialized in going out of business sales.

HEALTH CLUBS

There is certainly nothing inherently fraudulent about health clubs. The problem has not been in the concept of such clubs; the concept is usually a good one. The problem has been in the execution of the concept.

Some health clubs have sold memberships by making lavish representations about how the facility will develop or about future savings for the customer. But if those types of promises aren't contained in the written contract, they cannot be relied upon.

A typical high-pressure pitch to sell health club memberships will assure the consumer that the membership fee will double or triple unless they subscribe now. The fact is that the price will probably go consistently lower if memberships don't sell well at existing prices. Those contemplating joining a health club should be concerned about the full price of the membership and not just the seemingly affordable monthly fee, and should be alert for "extras" that are really essentials. Finally, they should be concerned about the financial backing of a health club. If a membership drive is just part of a "bust-out" scheme (See the section on Bust-Outs and Bankruptcy Frauds) or if the project lacks sufficient financing, the membership contract will be worthless when the club goes out of business. And to compound the problem the member may still be liable for payments to a financial institution that bought the credit contract from the club and is a holder in due course (See the section on Credit Capers). So be careful — for the sake of your mental health as well as your physical health.

HOME SOLICITATION SALES

The castle walls are breached and siege conditions exist when high-pressure salesmen hold the king and the royal family hostage. Ransom is the king's signature on a contract ordering storm windows, encyclopedias or magazines, to name a few products that are effectively peddled in the consumer's home. It is only then that calm returns to the castle — a calm that is shattered when:
1. The ordered product never arrives.
2. The product does not work.
3. The king realizes the price paid is several times the actual value of the item.

Most who engage in door-to-door solicitations subscribe to the philosophy that a product is sold, not bought.

And even assuming that the pitch put on the king's court is for a legitimate product, there are numerous problems to behold.

First there is no opportunity to compare price and quality with other similar products. And there is no time for sober reflection concerning whether or not the product is actually needed, or even wanted.

This problem is compounded when the product pitch is accompanied by an appeal to the sympathies of a purchaser. It seems that nearly everyone who sells certain products is (a) representing an unknown charity, (b) one sale away from a scholarship or (c) one sale away from a bonus that is an expense-paid trip to Hawaii.

There are many rules to follow when confronted by a door-to-door salesman. The paramount rule is to remember that it's your home. You are under no obligation to let the salesman enter, under no obligation to listen to his spiel and absolutely under no obligation to make a purchase. If he is obnoxious, ask him to leave. Never agree to make a purchase just to get rid of the pest. And never, never give him a check because there is a possibility that you might go ahead with the purchase. Some salesmen say this is necessary, telling you to contact them the next morning if you wish not to proceed with the purchase and your check will be returned immediately. In fact, the first thing in the morning your check is negotiated and the salesman moves on to his next conquest.

After the snake-oil salesman has your money, your recourses are few. There are monumental problems involved in locating him if he has perpetrated a scam and has vamoosed with the money. He may be subject to criminal prosecution but a trial without a defendant just isn't going to happen. And even if the product is legitimate, nondelivery and warranty work are exceedingly hard to come by when the manufacturer's plant is located at the opposite end of the country.

Legislative bodies have responded to this problem with passage of statutes that allow consumers a 72-hour period to cancel a contract that was entered into at the buyer's residence. The laws include certain exemptions, including exclusions for providing goods and services in an emergency and for goods and services primarily for agricultural use. The home solicitation contract must contain a "Buyer's Right To Cancel" clause. This does allow relief in certain circumstances. But it does *not* apply to any transaction that occurs at the seller's place of business. And it does not provide protection against absolutely fraudulent sales, because once money has changed hands you may legally be able to cancel the contract but if the seller cannot be located the legal right is of little practical value.

Castles in medieval times were protected by drawbridges and moats. Today when the moat is dry and the drawbridge lowered, the castle is subject to siege. Waging a Holy War after the battle has been lost to a glib-tongued talker does little to restore gold to the king's treasury.

Home solicitors who do not inform you of your three-day right to cancel or do not honor your exercise of that right should be reported to both the Federal Trade Commission and local law enforcement authorities.

MAGAZINE SUBSCRIPTIONS

They come in plagues like locusts covering your front door and eating away your privacy. Once inside the house their presentations are interminable and their prices high. Chances of delivery range from fair to nonexistent. Inevitably the pitch involves contracts that give you a cut rate on America's most popular magazines. And while a would-be scholarship winner is concluding a sale at your house, a companion down the street is espousing the benefits of having magazines available as part of a child's learning experience. Yet a third member of the crew is around the block pushing a sale in order to qualify for an expense-paid trip.

These pests are from the same family that produces door-to-door salespersons of all varieties; but magazine sales folks usually create a lower threshold of pain when incensed consumers try to rid their homes of this plague.

Actually magazine sales crews are frequently composed of young people who are recruited, trained and then transported far away from home where they are assigned blanket coverage of some areas. At the worst, members have unreasonably high quotas, are paid little or nothing and are shepherded by a company representative who does his best to keep the crew in line and working. Honesty is not the byword. Long-term contracts of one, two or three years are pushed with consumers paying hundreds of dollars for subscriptions to numerous magazines.

The distributor is generally located out-of-state and is very unresponsive to complaints. Sometimes magazines are in fact mailed to the subscriber and sometimes not. If not, theft prosecutions are extremely difficult because of the out-of-state status of the distributor and the difficulty in locating the salesman. A right to cancel the contract may exist but the distributor may ignore the cancellation and seldom makes refunds without intervention by a third party.

Even if the distributor is legitimate, that does not preclude the salesman from taking your money, tearing up the contract and never placing your order with the distributor, leaving you with a right of action against a salesman who cannot be found.

Nearly every gimmick known to man is utilized to attempt to sell magazines. Some of these include phony charity sponsorship, misrepresentations of all sorts and very high pressure tactics. At the very least anyone dealing with door-to-door magazine solicitors should never deal in cash. And contracts signed late at night without an opportunity for reflection or checking references are contracts that invite trouble.

There are no doubt organizations that offer legitimate discounts for purchasing several subscriptions. And there are no doubt legitimate (and even honest) door-to-door magazine solicitors. But the general rule absolutely has to be that it's safer to deal with the magazine publisher or some reputable distributor that you have checked upon. At least that way the odds are you'll get the magazines.

MAIL FRAUD

Anyone with any level of business sophistication understands that the U. S. mail is a vital artery of commerce in America. Billions of dollars of business is transacted annually through the mails. But where there is money there is fraud. The U. S. Postal Service estimates that at least $500 million per year is lost by consumers to perpetrators of fraudulent schemes that operate through the mails. Further, the Postal Service believes that the vast majority of these losses involve less than $15.00 per customer.

An examination of all the schemes that rely heavily on utilization of the mails would be impossible. They are as limitless as the imagination. Many of the most prevalent schemes are considered under separate sections of this book. Thus, in this section it is perhaps most beneficial to consider, in general, the types of schemes that are most conducive to the use of the mails, and to make some general observations about mail fraud.

If someone you never heard of called you on the telephone and told you that you would receive the opportunity of a lifetime for sending $15.00 to the caller but refused to tell you anything about the opportunity, you would undoubtedly be very skeptical and would probably not fall for the pitch. Yet for some unknown reason, the average person who reads about such a vague opportunity in a magazine or newspaper is much less skeptical and more likely to send in the money, without ever seeing the product involved or receiving any more information about it. This curious tendency to put undeserved faith in the written word is what makes fraudulent mail order schemes a veritable gold mine.

As a vehicle for perpetrating fraud the mails have many advantages. The lack of contact with the victim makes identification of the crooks difficult. The geographic distance between the victim and the perpetrator makes apprehension more difficult and more expensive. Finally, the small amount of money that is generally involved frequently causes the victim to chalk up the loss to experience rather than report it to postal authorities. Perhaps the only disadvantage to fraud by mail is the numerous legal devices available to postal inspectors and the U. S. Attorneys to bring mail schemes to a halt. The Postal Inspection Service is the investigatory and law enforcement arm of the U.S. Postal Service. Local and regional inspectors are listed in the phone book. Someone wishing to take a suspected fraud complaint to an inspector should retain all the information he can collect, including envelopes and other documentary evidence, relating to the questionable scheme.

By its very nature the mail is very suitable to the fostering of certain kinds of fraud and is the instrumental element of some schemes. What would a chain letter be without the mail? Chain referral schemes have long been successfully promoted by mail. Missing heir schemes could not be as effective without the use of official looking letters from allegedly legitimate sources. False billing schemes would surely fail if the phony bills were hand delivered. Work-at-home schemes and some fraudulent charitable solicitations rely on the mail to avoid the problems that would inevitably arise from personal contact. There could be no fraudulent correspondence courses without the correspondence aspect. The list of frauds that use the mails to some extent could go on and on.

The most common mail fraud scheme is the most simple. Fly-by-night operators advertise a product as available for purchase by mail order without any intent to provide the product, whether it be coins, stamps, magazines or some other item. It's imperative to investigate *before* you send in the money. Do some research to find out if the company is legitimate. Ask for a period of time to examine the product before paying for it. Another common situation is the mailing of a grossly inferior product after the mail order advertisement led you to believe you were getting a real bargain. One firm advertised emeralds for $5.00. Mail order purchasers got an emerald all right. An industrial grade emerald worth 50¢. Good for lining a fish tank.

One type of mail order fraud deserves special attention. The sale of worthless and sometimes dangerous "medicinal" products through the mail continues to be a serious problem. Advertising for the product preys upon human inadequacies and insecurities. The products are usually not expensive but they tend to be purchased by those who can least afford it. Whether it be pep pills, cures for obesity or aphrodisiacs, they are almost uniformly of no medical value. Sadly they are often a cause of delay in seeking beneficial medical treatment. If the "patient" were able to overcome his insecurities long enough to be objective, such products could never sell. Even the product names belie any notion of authenticity. Names like "Dr. Frederick's Fat-Away Pills" and "Athena Ultra Desire Cream" are inherently suspect. (*See also* the section on Medical Frauds.)

When it comes to purchasing products through the mail, be suspicious of any business that does not allow you to inspect the product before paying for it. In fact you can never be too suspicious. If it sounds too good to be true — it is.

UNORDERED MERCHANDISE (A GIFT TO YOU)

The package arrives in the mail addressed to you. It contains lifetime light bulbs, hosiery guaranteed not to run or a key-light that lights up the night. And it also contains a statement of the amount due on the product (plus postage and handling). You are sure that you didn't order the merchandise but you go ahead and pay the bill. By so doing you have become the victim of a merchandising fraud.

The actual value of the merchandise is always far less than you paid. And, more importantly, you have no obligation to pay for the merchandise even though you retain it. Generally, unordered merchandise can be retained as a gift with no obligation on the part of the recipient to accept it, return it or pay for it. Further, many states have statutes that make it a crime for the sender to mail a bill for any unsolicited goods, or for the sender to make any dunning communications.

A variation of this fraud is a scheme that induces the customer to order the merchandise. In this setup a coupon generally appears offering the product at a bargain price of $1.00. Some 30 to 60 days after receipt of the merchandise the consumer receives a demand letter from a collection agency seeking a "balance due" of $4.95. A large number of customers pay the balance to "protect their credit ratings."

In actuality the product is worth 49¢ so the initial dollar sent in with the order gives the seller a 100-percent profit. And that profit margin is increased dynamically with the next payment of $4.95 — especially when one considers that the only expense in collecting it is the cost of paper and envelope and the cost of the "collection agency" maintaining an answering service.

The answering service is usually in New York City or Los Angeles and all "collections" are made out-of-state, thus tremendously complicating any proceedings that might be brought by residents of Nevada or Rhode Island.

Solution: Keep all unordered merchandise as a gift. (If you feel thankful an appropriately worded card of thanks can be sent to the sender.) And report bogus collection operations to authorities as well as ignoring the demand to pay. Should the collection agency in fact follow through on its threat to report negative credit information concerning your credit rating you generally have a right to correct erroneous information or to include your version of the transaction in the credit agency files.

Caveat: Be sure not to use this procedure when you did order the merchandise, when it is replacement merchandise for items you in fact ordered or for ordered merchandise when a dispute later arises over its quality. There may be a remedy in such situations, but it is not considering the merchandise to be a gift.

VACATION FRAUDS

A four-day, three-night trip to Las Vegas, with hotel accommodations, two shows, and $300.00 in gambling chips — all for only $35.00. What a deal! Too good to pass up, right? Maybe not.

Many people have very sad stories to tell about the vacation packages they purchased. Some have gotten to the destination only to find that their reservations were not honored. Others have found the vacation package was not applicable during the time of the year or days of the week they went. Others have found so many hidden costs that a nonpackaged vacation would have been cheaper. Still others have sent in their money and never heard from the company again.

There are many legitimate vacation packages available. The task is to determine with whom you are dealing. First of all consider what comprises a vacation package. Generally, a marketing company approaches hotels and other tourist facilities and contracts with them to market vacation packages. The tourist facility is quite willing to offer reduced rates because their interest is to secure business during the off season or slow part of the week, or in the case of Las Vegas for instance to attract gamblers into their casino where they'll spend enough money to make the package very profitable for the hotel. Therefore you should recognize at the outset that, regardless of what a promoter tells you, no one is giving anything away and no one has won anything. The package is being offered to you because everybody makes money off the deal — including the promoter.

If you're interested in a vacation package being offered contact an agency, such as the Better Business Bureau or the Chamber of Commerce, in the vacation city. Determine if the company promoting the package is well established and reliable and determine the quality of the hotel involved. Then contact the hotel and confirm their relationship to the vacation package promoter. You can never be too careful. It may prevent a dream vacation from turning into a nightmare.

Time sharing vacation programs are being enthusiastically promoted as the ideal solution to the problem of keeping down vacation costs. For a lump sum of, say, $10,000.00 you can buy an interest in a condominium in Hawaii for one week a year for twenty-five years. You can even trade your week in Hawaii for a week in the Colorado ski country if you so desire. Sounds delightful. And it can be — if the operation is on a sufficiently sound financial basis to provide assurance it will be around next year, let alone twenty-five years from now. Your one-week-a-year interest in a complex in foreclosure won't be worth much.

Don't be so blinded by a salesman's description of a perpetual vacation paradise that you forget to ask questions or receive answers concerning the company or companies involved and their success or failure in other ventures. Investigate the situation fully and have a trusted financial counselor scrutinize the investment.

WHOLESALE BUYER'S CLUB

If you pay a little, you can save a lot — or so the organizers would have you believe. There are actually two ways in which you can be victimized by wholesale buyer's clubs. The first is when the club is being organized. Investors are sought to buy into the corporation, which will establish the Wholesale Discount Club of America. In return for the investment each will receive not only tremendous benefits in purchasing products but also a percentage of the profits. Or perhaps they will receive exclusive rights to market memberships within a specified geographical area.

There are numerous variations but usually someone well known in a community is brought into the initial cadre to lend credibility to the organization. Sometimes this individual does make fairly large sums of money and sometimes he is paid in promises. In either event when the promoters who recruited him move on, the local organizer is left to face the lawsuits that almost inevitably follow, even assuming that no criminal liability exists. And possibilities in that area abound. The sales of interests in the yet-to-be-formed club may be defined as violations of security laws. The sales to individuals in designated areas may be merely a thinly disguised pyramid promotion. The list goes on and on. But in this version the club is formed and only investors are victimized.

Version two offers something for everyone. Whatever you wish to purchase can be obtained for you through the Wholesale Buyer's Club of North America which, because of its volume buying power, offers discounts ranging from 15 to 75 percent. Your only obligation is to purchase a membership in "the fastest growing money-saving club in America." The cost of membership is $300.00 plus a fee of $25.00 per year to cover bookkeeping expenses. As an added inducement to join you are offered a bonus, which in itself is valued (it is said) at over $300.00. Bonuses may be silverware, dishes or a stereo set (which has an actual value of $99.49 — maybe). The salesman also shows you bargain items that can be bought at tremendous savings. How can you lose? You sign up. And a month later when you attempt to buy merchandise, you find that the prices are no lower than the prices in local stores. Many of the items that you request, or that the salesman guaranteed would be available, are not offered through the club. Frequently, there are long delays and price changes on the limited items that you can purchase. When you contact the home office one of two things occurs:

1. You are ignored.
2. Shortages are said to be only temporary and in the interim the club has available a coupon book for obtaining discounts locally. The book sells for $125.00 and the coupons are valid for 18 months. By then, you are assured, the club's temporary problems will have been resolved. And they usually are. The club ceases doing business and the principals move elsewhere to form the Wholesale Buyer's Club of the West.

3

Repair Frauds and Home Improvement Schemes (The Art of Compounding Your Problems)

AUTOMOBILE REPAIR FRAUD

Ask anyone who has spent some time in the business of fielding consumer complaints what the single greatest source of complaints is and the response will almost certainly be automobile repairs. Ask the same person what type of consumer complaint is the greatest source of frustration for those who attempt to resolve complaints and the response will probably be the same — automobile repairs. The fact is that those who feel victimized by automobile repair facilities are often motivated to complain but unfortunately are seldom in a position to adequately support their accusations.

There is no doubt that millions of dollars are spent annually on unnecessary auto repairs. Part of this economic waste is due to incompetence, but much of it is due to fraud. Like every business the auto repair business has its bad apples. In the past decade state legislatures have begun to react to public pressure by passing statutes designed to curb abuses. The auto repair legislation now enacted in several states typically involves the right to written estimates, record keeping requirements, the right to have replaced parts returned, repossession rights for the garage and criminal penalties for noncompliance with the statutory requirements. The last several years have also seen improvement in the ability of law enforcement agencies to conduct undercover investigations that can lead to the successful prosecution of automobile repair fraud.

The most common form of auto repair fraud is "low-balling," a practice that exists in many businesses involving repairs of mechanical devices. Here's a typical scenario. The customer brings his car in knowing something is wrong but not knowing exactly what is wrong. The mechanic's preliminary finding is that the problem is not serious. The customer is told the car will be available tomorrow. No sooner does the customer get home or back to the office than the phone rings. It's the garage telling him that upon closer examination the problem is a serious one that will cost at least $450.00 to fix. The customer has a choice: Pay the $450.00 or pay to have the car reassembled but unrepaired. If he refuses to pay the garage for reassembly the garage will assert a lien on the car and refuse to release it. The problem is described as being quite dangerous and one requiring immediate attention. The tendency is to trust the mechanic and not to undergo the inconvenience of getting "another opinion." The result may well be that the customer pays hundreds of dollars for unnecessary repairs.

The best protection against low-balling is to find a repair shop that has stood the test of time. Shops that have a list of long-standing loyal customers are the best bet. Written estimates also provide some protection against unnecessary repairs. They should not be waived. Asking for the return of replaced parts can also prevent fraud.

Even if you can't prove your suspicion that you've been the victim of auto repair fraud, report your suspicions to law enforcement. Enough complaints of a similar nature may cause an agency to undertake an investigation of the auto repair facility. An expert mechanic can examine a car and ensure that it is in excellent working condition and then intentionally induce a minor malfunction. If the car is then taken into a garage and an attempt is made to sell a major repair, a fraud case may result. This investigating technique has been particularly successful in the detection of fraud in the transmission repair business. Transmission repair is an area most conducive to fraud for the simple reason that there are at least a dozen malfunctions not having to do with the transmission that are manifested by erratic shifting. The average person, with no knowledge about cars, will generally conclude that the shifting problem is indicative of a transmission problem. Thus he is ripe to be sold an expensive but unnecessary transmission repair job.

Perhaps the most insidious form of auto repair fraud is that which may await the traveler who visits a service station along the highway en route to his destination. Stations that do not rely on repeat business are the most likely to succumb to the temptation to engage in sabotage of cars as a way to increase profits. When the customer pulls into a service station after four hours of driving, the kids typically run off to find a Coke machine while Mom and Dad look for the rest rooms. Meanwhile the service station attendant has an opportunity to puncture a tire with an icepick, slash a fanbelt or radiator hose, drop Alka Seltzer in the battery or dribble fluid on the ground to make it appear that the shock absorbers are leaking. The sabotage will either make the car inoperable or make it appear that the car is too dangerous to drive. In any event the customer is far from home in alien territory and is likely to have the repair work done right there. Service station attendants who sabotage cars in this manner are called "50 percenters" because they typically have an arrangement with the station owner whereby they receive 50 percent of the profit from the purchase of new parts due to the sabotage.

If a service station swindler is not in a real devious mood he may simply "pour oil" from an empty oil can into the engine and charge the customer for it. Or he may bend a windshield wiper so it is inoperable and point it out to the customer when he returns from the rest room.

Before you leave on vacation have your car thoroughly checked by your local mechanic. When you drive into a service station while traveling *never* leave the car unattended. Don't sit in the car either. Get out and watch the attendant like a hawk. If the attendant suggests that major repairs are necessary take the time to double-check at another auto repair facility.

The auto repair business is essentially the same as most businesses in America. The majority of the people in it are honest. But there are those who will gouge you for a buck every chance they get. Don't give them the chance. Take the time to educate yourself about cars, and about repair shops in your locality. It may save you time, trouble, and money.

ENERGY SAVING FRAUDS

Energy conservation in the operation of a motor vehicle or in heating or cooling your home or place of business may be accomplished by certain well-recognized practices, including keeping a vehicle properly tuned and insulating your home or place of business.

But contrary to the advertising claims regarding many energy saving devices there is no inexpensive "wonder product" that will increase your gas mileage 50 percent or cut back your home heating bill by a phenomenal 60 percent.

Persons or firms that sell such products are really not concerned with the results you obtain. Those grandiose promises are merely so many words written upon the wind.

Take, for example, the gasoline additive that promises up to 12 miles more per gallon and costs only $2.95. It has to be added to your gas tank only twice a month. Certain additives may in fact slightly improve gasoline mileage; but that full-sized vehicle which normally gets 12 miles per gallon is not going to suddenly get twice that much. And many of the additives may in fact be harmful to your engine, resulting in lower mileage and larger repair bills.

You should be cautious of what you put into your gasoline or oil and should check with a qualified mechanic before using the product. The same holds true of any replacement part or engine modification that claims fantastic results in gas savings.

After you have been driven into "saving" energy in your automobile, there is someone who wishes to compound your good fortune by saving you additional dollars at your home or place of business. These "experts" will normally operate on the frontiers of existing technology, making it difficult to check their claims.

As an example consider solar heating. There is no question but that solar heating can save money when compared to conventional heating. But a solar heating system can cost several thousand dollars for installation and may have disadvantages in certain regions. That makes no difference to the fraud perpetrator. He promises a new advance in technology, a greatly reduced cost and nearly instant installation. For $1,500.00 he will put a system in your home that will save you twice that amount within four years.

He presents impressive credentials to you including a degree from M.I.T. and copies of articles he has authored that have been published in major magazines. He takes a down payment of $1,000.00 and that (if you are lucky) is the last you ever see of him. If you are unfortunate, he will attempt to install the system, which turns out to be very crude. Water leaks through your roof where he improperly sealed the space between the unit and the hole he cut in your roof.

The unit itself works — at least well enough to concentrate heat on your roof (in much the way that a magnifying glass works on a leaf) and your home goes up in flames.

Of course when you check on his credentials, the degree from M.I.T. is forged as are the by-lines on the articles.

The same types of problems can exist with insulation, other alternate heating systems, storm windows or whatever is being touted as the energy saving advance of the century. And even when a product, such as storm windows, can legitimately save you money, the price charged may well be far in excess of what you can buy the product for elsewhere.

This is especially true of those merchants who utilize boiler room techniques to telephone everyone in the community (two or three times) pushing storm windows, insulation or other products, or who peddle such products, unsolicited, at your door.

Before being sucked in, it is always wise to obtain several quotes on products and installation. Check on performance claims and be wary of phenomenal claims. Also be sure to check and see if the installation is done properly.

These steps could save you time, money, irritation and perhaps your home.

FREE INSPECTION FRAUDS

Many businesses in various lines of work offer to conduct free inspections to determine if repairs or services are required for the item inspected. Unfortunately many consumers have a naive notion that the businessman is performing such free inspections out of the kindness of his heart and view it as a real sacrifice on his part. Stop and ask yourself how a business can afford to continually conduct free inspections. There's really no mystery. It does it because the inspections lead to higher profits — from the sale of services and parts because of problems diagnosed in the inspection. The potential for fraud becomes readily apparent. Whether it involves an inspection of appliances, of an automobile, of the furnace or for rodent or insect infestation, the inspection will be anything but free if the inspector manages to convince you to pay for unnecessary repairs or services. You may be better off calling an established business that charges reasonable rates for inspections or routine servicing.

Although free inspections should always be viewed skeptically, the mere fact that a business offers to perform free inspections in its advertising does not necessarily mean that it survives by performing unnecessary work. Many businesses of long standing in a community might offer free inspections because they have learned that enough legitimate work will result to make the free inspections cost-effective. Therefore you might look for other danger signals, such as an unsolicited offer to conduct a free inspection.

The essence of most free inspection fraud schemes is a door-to-door, mail or telephone solicitation. If someone comes to your door and offers to conduct a free inspection of your furnace, stop and think for a moment. If this outfit had any legitimacy, wouldn't it have enough work to do without soliciting door-to-door to do free inspections? The odds are excellent that it's a scam perpetrated by highly transient sorts that won't be in town a week later. Politely refuse any unsolicited offer to conduct a free inspection.

While some situations require periodic routine inspection and servicing, others do not. A termite inspection just for the sake of having a termite inspection might be an invitation to a smooth talker to convince you that you've got a problem when you really don't. In such cases arrange for an inspection only when you think you've got a problem.

If you always remember that businesses exist to make money you'll be less apt to fall prey to a free inspection fraud. Dealing with a well-established business with a good reputation is your best bet.

HOME REPAIR FRAUDS

The castle is continually under siege by the Huns of Home Repair. These soldiers of disrepute have made a science of separating you from your money and leaving your house in a shambles. There are really two varieties of "contractors" who perform this "service" for you, the incompetent and the dishonest. Either variety can cost you thousands of dollars.

First the incompetent variety:

This individual or firm is like the shade tree mechanic next door who helps you work on your car. After the work is done, sometimes the vehicle runs and sometimes it has to be towed away. The problem with home repair is that you can't tow your home to a qualified mechanic. Usually the incompetent contractor's price is cheaper than others and usually he wants the bulk of the price up front "to pay for materials." The contracts he has the homeowner sign are half-sheets of paper that provide him with a modicum of protection while giving the homeowner nothing in return. Almost inevitably this contractor uses your money to pay for materials and subcontractors' labors on past jobs. Eventually this process of robbing Peter to pay Paul becomes dysfunctional, at which time the last homeowners on the ladder lose when the contractor declares bankruptcy. And during the process many homeowners find that liens have been attached to their property by subcontractors who have not been paid by the contractor. The lien holder can and will foreclose on the property if his claim is not satisfied. The result is that the homeowner pays twice for the same job. Frequently the job was not completed or was substandard. Again the homeowner pays twice.

Depending upon the laws in the state where you reside, it is probable that the incompetent contractor described above has not committed a crime. It simply is not a crime to be a bad businessman and debtors' prisons no longer exist. The remedy for the homeowner then is to sue the contractor and obtain a judgment. The catch is that the judgment has little value if the contractor has no assets. And since the contractor has no criminal liability he is free to move to another area and start the same borderline business all over again.

There is no sure protection against this type contractor but one can lessen the probabilities of becoming entangled with him.

1. Demand references. Check with people for whom the contractor has previously worked. Was the work satisfactory? Was the warranty honored? Were any liens filed?
2. How long has the contractor been in business in the community?
3. What are his financial resources? Is the business stable?
4. Is the contractor bonded and licensed?

Be sure that an attorney examines any contract involving repairs *before* you sign — his fee might seem large but it is very small in comparison to the thousands of dollars you might otherwise lose.

Also, keep track of monies paid in advance of job completion. Demand that they be placed into an escrow account and disbursed only for payment for materials and work completed by subcontractors. Demand proof of payment of these bills as the job progresses and check to see if they have in fact been paid.

Last, make arrangements if possible to withhold a portion of the final payment for 30 to 90 days after completion to insure that latent defects do not develop during that time. If you have an honest contractor he will have no problem with conducting his business in a fair and businesslike manner.

You have now at least ruled out dealing with the absolute fly-by-night businessman. Problems may still develop but your odds are tremendously improved.

Now, the dishonest contractor:

This breed of criminal is epitomized by the "Terrible Williamson Gang" that operates nationwide. Each spring the members of the gang climb into their pickups which have side racks, ladders and changeable signs, and spread out across the country spending no more than a few days in any area.

A typical approach: One of the members of the gang comes to your door and tells you he has noticed that your driveway needs repair. "We were just in the neighborhood on another driveway job and we had some material left over. I can give you a real good price on the job just so I can get rid of the excess material." And the price is cheap. It's less than half of prices you've previously been quoted so you jump at the chance. He and a helper do the job and as he's leaving he tells you not to drive on it for two or three days as it has to "cure." You pay him and he drives away. As luck would have it, the rains come the next day; you look out and find that your gorgeous driveway is gone — it has washed onto your previously green grass. All the contractor did was spray a mixture of black paint and alcohol onto the drive. It glistened and looked gorgeous but served absolutely no legitimate purpose. You are incensed and call authorities. There is no question that a crime has been committed but a prosecution is unlikely. The gang uses hit-and-run tactics and is in the next state by the time you discover the fraud. You find you know nothing about them and that you can't even identify the person who took you. You're not alone. He and his compatriots have been all over town doing driveways, painting houses and repairing roofs. They leave several thousand dollars richer with existing defects not repaired. For the roofs they repaired they may have used the same paint-based compound they sprayed on driveways. The house paint is whitewash that has been thinned down to the point that only the color is left. It too washes off in the rain.

The Williamsons are notorious but others have followed their pattern. They can all be easily foiled if the homeowner is even moderately cautious.

1. Do not contract without checking with the Better Business Bureau or other entity.
2. Never pay the full amount in advance. Work will probably not be done and you will be unable to locate the contractor.
3. Ask for and check references.
4. Be wary of the door-to-door solicitor, especially if he just happens to have materials left over.
5. Distrust the contractor who tells you that your home will be a "sample" or if he offers you discounts for finding him other customers.
6. Do not give in to high-pressure tactics designed to force you into making an immediate decision.
7. Warning lights should flash if the price is *too* cheap. Hardly anyone does work for nothing.

Being so careful may sound like an unnecessary hassle, but it's the type of hassle that can pay huge returns in dollars and aggravation saved.

SWIMMING POOL RACKETS

Most of us will never buy a swimming pool and need not concern ourselves with schemes that prey on those fortunate enough to be in the market for pools. But for those who live in warmer climes where pools are standard equipment, swimming pool rackets are a very real problem.

The most typical scheme is very simple. A new contractor comes to town and advertises a bargain price for swimming pool construction as a "grand opening" promotion. The customer pays no less than one-half of the total price "up front" and the remainder upon completion. The contractor digs the hole, which is the quickest and least expensive part of the job. In fact, he digs holes for all the customers under contract in an assembly line approach as opposed to a one pool at a time approach, saying that is what keeps his price so reasonable. But he never gets much further and eventually closes up shop and moves on without finishing the job or even delivering the necessary materials. He has taken at least half the money for about a quarter of the work. The customer is inclined to suspect that a financial failure by the contractor has caused the situation. But it was a setup from the start. In fact, the scheme may involve a "bust-out" or planned bankruptcy. (*See* the section on Bust-Outs and Bankruptcy Frauds.)

Other schemes might involve "above the ground" pools. They may be touted as maintenance free, highly durable or suitable for a skating rink in winter, when in fact they are of grossly inferior quality. The 90-day warranty expires before the ravages of winter destroy the pool.

The same advice applies here as applies in an attempt to avoid most home improvement frauds. Deal with a reputable firm that has stood the test of time and remember that the cheapest deal may not be the best. The quality of materials is of the greatest importance in swimming pool construction.

TELEVISION REPAIR FRAUD

As a society we are watching more and more television. Unfortunately we are not experiencing a proportional increase in our knowledge of the mechanical workings of television sets. So when the set malfunctions we remain almost totally at the mercy of the repairman. This fact makes us very vulnerable to the dishonest TV repairman.

The first opportunity for dishonesty occurs before any repairs are undertaken. A repairman who is called to a home to fix a TV set may falsely claim that the set cannot be fixed in the home and must be taken into the shop. He doesn't tell you until you get the bill that he charges a considerable transportation fee and "bench fee" for work done in the shop. In fact the guy who came out to your house may not even be a repairman at all but rather a driver who receives a commission for each set he manages to get into the shop.

Most TV repairs can be done in the home. If the person who comes out says it can't be fixed at home ask him for a written work estimate based on his examination in your home. Also question him concerning any fees that will be assessed for taking the set into the shop. If such fees are charged, transport it yourself.

The practice of "low-balling," discussed in the section on Automobile Repair Fraud, is also prevalent in the TV repair business. You may be told upon first inspection of your set that the problem seems minor and that you can pick up your set the next morning. No sooner do you get home or back to the office than the repairman calls to tell you that upon examining the inside of the set more closely the problem is extensive — and expensive. Chances are you'll trust the guy and you won't go through the trouble of getting a second opinion. Chances are you'll be buying unnecessary parts and unnecessary repairs. Asking for written estimates and for the return of replaced parts are ways to protect yourself against low-balling. But the best way is to carefully shop around for a repair shop that has earned a good reputation over a period of several years.

Television repair fraud schemes can be creative. In one such scheme, a repairman called to homes to fix malfunctioning sets during the spring and summer months always diagnosed the problem as internal damage caused by lightning (which can occur on occasion). He would always quote a price of $185.00 for repairs but inform the customer that a claim could be made under the customer's homeowner's insurance policy. The scheme was uncovered when insurance companies reported to local authorities that a disproportionate number of claims for lightning damage were being filed in that area. In an undercover investigation authorities took a single tube out of an otherwise properly functioning set and called the suspect repairman. When he diagnosed the problem as lightning damage on three successive occasions he was arrested and later convicted of fraud.

4

Self-Improvement Schemes (Your Dreams Can Cost You Money)

BODY AND BOSOM BUILDING SCHEMES

There is no easy way to build your body, despite what promoters of many body building programs may claim. Even when body building is attempted through strict diet and strenuous exercise there are limitations on what can be accomplished. The extent of success may depend upon your natural frame.

So whether you happen to be a "98-pound weakling" or an Olive Oyl, there is no company that can turn you into an instant Charles Atlas or Marilyn Monroe. The claims can be fantastic and the means to that end may include pills, lotions, newly discovered exercise programs or a visit to a spa. The fact is that if "instant" results are promised, the program is almost certainly a fraud and will not result in your being able to kick sand in the bully's face or represent your state in the Miss America Pageant. The only "instant" successes are brought about, at least in the area of bosom building, through surgical implantation or through silicone injections. If not done properly these techniques can result in horrendous disfigurations as well as a variety of lifelong health problems. As in most areas, the perpetrator of the fraud is not concerned with long-range problems, health or otherwise. He has obtained his objective once you have paid a high price for the product or service.

Usually the instant results are promised with regard to products ordered by mail. The first rule in this area is to be extremely suspicious of products available only by mail order.

The second rule is to never undertake a body building program without first consulting a reputable doctor who can determine your state of health and also advise you on reasonable limitations to what you may achieve.

There is absolutely no substitute for proper diet and exercise regardless of the phenomenal claims made in advertisements.

DANCE STUDIO RACKETS

Complaints about deceptive and unfair practices in the dancing lesson business seem to be cyclical in nature. Every few years they crop up as a significant problem. Then, after a few of the fly-by-night outfits go under, the problem dies down for a while.

The practices most frequently complained about have typically been aimed at the elderly and, more often than not, widows. They include high-pressure sales tactics aimed at getting the consumer's signature on a contract that involves a ludicrous number of lessons and an unconscionable amount of money, which is generally payable over a long period of time — with considerable interest. The victim is typically subjected to a presentation that blinds him to the true costs of the contract. The salesman may exploit the victim's need for companionship by exaggerating the social ramifications involved. Other common ploys are to misrepresent the quality of instruction, the availability of refunds, the number of people taking lessons and the potential of the students to become expert dancers themselves.

The fact of the matter is that a consumer wishing to take dance lessons can learn a basic curriculum of dance steps in a relatively short period of time and at a reasonable cost. Lessons given by church, school or community groups may be much preferable in terms of cost and companionship to the expensive commercial dance studio. If you do choose to take lessons through a dance studio, review the contract very carefully so you know exactly what you're getting and what you are paying for it. Determine the reputation of the business involved and the length of time it's been around.

Dance studios may also prey on the psychology of parents who envision their child as a ballet star, soaking them for thousands of dollars. The psychological ploys utilized, as well as the warning signs and precautions, are generally the same as those discussed in the section of this book on Talent Agency Frauds.

EDUCATION COURSES

For $15.00 and a stamp you can become a Ph.D. Or, if you desire, there are courses that will teach you how to become a disc jockey or how to drive a semitruck. The Ph.D. offer is an out-and-out fraud. The courses may be. There are numerous "schools" from which one may order everything from an Associate of Arts Degree to a Doctor of Divinity. Some of these entities profess a course of study that must be completed prior to award of the degree. In actuality the only requirement is the ability to write a check to the school.

Usually the cost increases with the level of education you desire to attain. A few of these "schools" do in fact offer a course of study that you may complete in your home. The problem is that the "school" has no qualified instructors and may well be run by a paroled con. Upon completion you receive a degree but the school is certainly not accredited. Many others merely issue diplomas that are copies of legitimate degrees awarded by highly respected universities.

If you do not desire to attain a degree, there is a trade school beckoning you. These schools "guarantee" graduates well-paying jobs as airline mechanics, computer programmers, airline cabin attendants, over-the-road trucking, U. S. or state civil servants, or beauticians, to name but a few of the thousands of occupations for which you can prepare. These trade schools and "institutions of higher learning" are not to be confused with the real thing. You do *earn* a degree from an accredited college or university. And good (even prestigious) trade schools graduate people particularly qualified to earn a living in a specialty trade.

The two types can be easily differentiated. Check to see that what is being promised does in fact exist. Sales presentations often imply that you will receive professional training, housing while attending the "institute" and guaranteed placement upon graduation. After succumbing to the high-pressure tactics and paying substantial fees you may find the training is inadequate, the housing does not exist and postgraduation jobs are no easier to find than before you attended the school.

Other trade schools, such as a beauty school or a diesel mechanic training school, are designed to earn tuition money for the operation and also to provide a no-cost source of labor. High-school graduates are often solicited to enroll. In addition to tuition each is required to purchase a kit that includes the basic tools of the trade. These can usually be acquired elsewhere at a much cheaper cost. The course is "taught" with students working upon individuals (or their vehicles) under the supervision of a teacher. Actually the school could enroll the student, provide free tuition, room and board and still make a profit from customers' fees. Again the guaranteed placement upon graduation never comes to fruition. A variation on this scheme is the high-school diploma mill for those wishing to complete their basic education. Tuition is usually expensive but the results are cheap since the diploma may not be worth anything. The diploma mill, you learn later, is not accredited.

When considering pursuing any of the above courses of study, check to see if the institution is accredited and by whom. If a license is required by the state, has it been obtained? Also check with the local Board of Education to see what programs and vocational courses are available through the local school district. And be extremely careful of opportunities heavily advertised in the want ads. They may be legitimate but prestigious institutions usually have waiting lists and do not need to advertise.

If all you want is a $15.00 Ph.D., these opportunities are for you. Most people, however, can't afford to invest several thousand dollars to obtain a worthless piece of paper — especially when the investment represents their only chance to improve poor economic opportunities.

FORTUNE-TELLING FRAUDS

You are seated across the table from a young woman who is dressed in a peasant-style blouse and long skirt. She has a bandana on her head. This is the fifth visit you have made; the first was occasioned by curiosity. At that first visit, Gifted Jane revealed to you that you are facing personal problems relating to an inheritance you received from a relative you never really liked.

Now Jane tells you to repeat after her:

"You say God"
"God"
"Destroy this evil"
"Destroy this evil"
"Put it in there. No more bad luck"
"No more bad luck"
"No more suffering"
"No more suffering"
"To come my way"
"To come my way"
"You say Dear God"
"Dear God"
"Hear me out loud"
"Hear me out loud"

"Help me to get rid of this bad luck"
"Help me to get rid of this bad luck"
"To get rid of this darkness"
"To get rid of this darkness"
"Hear my wishes"
"Hear my wishes"
"Hear my prayers"
"Hear my prayers"
"Help me"
"Help me"
"And guide me"
"And guide me"
"Through this work"
"Through this work"
"Thank you"
"Thank you"
"For sending me to the sister"
"For sending me to the sister"
"To get rid of this evil"
"To get rid of this evil"
"No more suffering"
"No more suffering"
"No more darkness"
"No more darkness"
"To come my way"
"To come my way"
"I want to have happiness"
"I want to have happiness"
"Instead of"
"Instead of"
"The people"
"The people"
"To put the white sheet"
"To put the white sheet"
"Over one of my family's face"
"Over one of my family's face"
"Let me put it on this face"
"Let me put it on this face"
"Cause it to take all the suffering"
"Cause it to take all the suffering"
"It can take all of the misery"
"It can take all of the misery"

Jane speaks with a heavy accent reminiscent of the Count Dracula movies dialogue.

"You trust me?"
"I do."

"You understand that this must be secret, that you can't tell anyone or the evil cannot be removed?"
You nod.

Gifted Jane, satisfied with the day's labors, sends you home with instructions to take a tomato, place it in your right shoe and keep it under your bed overnight.

"You must come back tomorrow and bring the tomato."

She wishes you well and sends you on your way. The next day, tomato in hand, you reappear.

"You follow my instructions?"
"Yes."

Jane takes the tomato and covers it with a cloth. She then places it on the floor and has you stomp on it. She stirs the resultant mess and a devil's head is found in the midst of the remnants.

"See that! See that! That's the evil but its appearance means I can help you."

And help you she does. Gifted Jane determines the evil is attached to the ill-gotten inheritance. In order to lift the evil you are going to have to burn your money.

On one occasion you bring in $10,000.00. Jane matches it with $10,000.00 of her money and wraps the package in a white cloth. She then burns the packet. Or she may tell you it's necessary to bury the money. The instructions are as follows:

You must take all the money (yours and hers) and go to the cemetery at 3:00 A.M. You must go in the nude and you will be met there by nine spirits who will speak to you in nine languages. After answering their questions, each in his own tongue, you must bury the money.

"You understand?"
"Yes."
"Will you do this thing?"
"Yes."
"How many languages do you speak?"
"One or two."
"Then how you going to understand the spirits?"
"I don't know."

Eventually Jane tells you she knows the languages and she will go for you. You ask if you can go along.

"No. You go or I go. We no can go together."

So you give her the money to lift the evil spirits and she instead lifts the money just as she did with the burning episode. You were upset enough that you didn't notice that the packets were switched. All she did was burn a package of play money.

The above encounter is a composite of very real episodes. Gifted Jane is really gifted. If you go in for a fortune telling, she will take your $5.00 or $10.00 and return a canned spiel. If you appear to be a promising prospect she will burn a candle for you at a cost of $30.00 or more.

She'll make an appointment for you to return and over a period of time she will find devil's heads, snakes or clumps of hair in tomatoes or eggs. She may even slay a chicken for you, all in a ritualistic manner combined with incantations. She builds a level of trust and she then begins to bilk you. Almost always she will leave you a small part of your money. And most likely when you later analyze the scam, you will not report it because of fear or shame.

If you incessantly demand a refund, it is likely you will receive at least partial repayment. The last thing Gifted Jane wants is publicity and the involvement of law enforcement. Both are very bad for business.

Gifted Jane has half a dozen names and has lived in at least as many cities. She is an excellent amateur psychologist and preys on normal feelings, using your vulnerabilities to her best advantage.

Various victims provide everything to Gifted Jane including personal clothing, furniture, groceries and clothing for her children. It's necessary to bring these items to her to help remove the evil.

Each of us smirks, "But that could never happen to me. It's all too silly."

Perhaps.

But each of us is vulnerable to some sort of con game. And more than a few of us, at certain times in our lives, are desperate enough to be vulnerable to Gifted Jane.

She spends her life polishing her craft and you may well become a victim if you visit her place of business.

In fact the odds are nearly 100 percent. She may only get $5.00 for a "palm reading" but she will get at least that much. And you could be victimized for far more. Amounts in the thousands of dollars are not uncommon. The only sure protection is not to enter her establishment.

Remember the old nursery rhyme that begins, "Come into my parlor, said the spider to the fly."

SONG SHARKS AND VANITY PUBLISHERS

If you would like to become a published author or to have your songs published, these firms are for you. Or at least the firms will attempt to convince you that's the case. In both cases, promoters promise to publish your work. They'll certainly do that — and nothing more. The cost will be borne entirely by you, the author. It's a great deal, if you want to be published regardless of the cost and if you have an empty warehouse that needs to be filled with 10,000 copies of undying prose or records that never quite made the top 40. The firms will provide other services to you including distribution and promotion, but these services will cost you considerably more.

These alternatives may well be profitable under certain circumstances, but the author should be extremely careful in dealing with such firms. As a general rule if the work has sufficient merit a publisher will undertake the task of publishing, promotion and distribution at his expense, paying you a percentage of the profits. You may not make any money but under those circumstances you at least do not spend thousands of dollars and assume all of the risk.

Once you have a work published by the vanity publisher or the song shark, he has made his profit. Whether or not the work sells is immaterial to him as he generally does not expect to make money based on sales. Thus his incentive to promote the work is seriously diminished.

What you really receive are copies of your work in published form, copies that cost much more than simply the printing and paper costs. The only advantage is that the publisher has the capabilities of providing printing, promotion and distribution, all of which are available through separate firms, sometimes at far less cost.

One other problem is that vanity publishers and song sharks often accept virtually anything for publication. The criterion is not the quality of the work but the size of the author's pocketbook. Thus even the true great American novel or the song of the century is diminished in stature and tainted by this kind of publisher.

Generally the cost far outweighs any benefit. Consequently, song sharks and vanity publishers should be avoided unless all else fails and you have a compulsive desire to be published. If you can afford to satisfy that desire, by all means proceed. But remember it will be at your own risk.

TALENT AGENCY FRAUDS

Each of us has a desire for attention. For some this desire is satisfied by family members. Others require more and are satisfied only by the plaudits bestowed by an entire community. And for still others, all the world's a stage.

People in all of these categories, but most especially those in the latter, are susceptible to talent agency frauds, which generally are initiated through an advertisement in the local newspapers offering one a screen test, a modeling agency contract or an evaluation of one's performing potential.

The variations on this theme are innumerable. To list but a few we include:

1. The straight deception. Females are sought for modeling or acting capabilities. When they appear for the audition they are asked to disrobe. It turns out the advertiser is using the scam in an effort to obtain sexual favors or the job is that of a nude dancer in a local cabaret that has a high-class clientele composed of members of the Hell's Angels.
2. The prospective actor or actress is told he has a tremendous amount of talent. To develop it the person is told he has to sign up for a series of acting or modeling lessons with a guaranteed job at the end of the lessons in a Broadway play or posing on the cover of a major magazine.
3. Same as above except here the person's talent is so far advanced that lessons are not required. The only thing standing between the applicant and success is "someone who knows the business." Thus the applicant signs up for someone to act as agent for him or her and a flat monthly fee is charged rather than the standard commission because "in the long run that will save you a lot of money." Needless to say no jobs are ever obtained and the expenditures by the client are completely wasted.
4. The talent agency in this example preys upon the parents of precocious children, children who have average ability but whose parents believe them to have a tremendous amount of talent and children who have no talent but whose parents delude themselves concerning the child's ability. The parents pay thousands for lessons with no results. Perhaps one of every 25,000 children "makes it" but that is due only to the law of averages.
5. This variation can be conducted by talent or modeling agencies or by a separate "business" that conducts beauty pageants or talent pageants (i.e., The Miss Cutesy America Pageant). Upon close examination one finds that these "contestants" pay large sums of money or enhance their chances to win by obtaining required publicity for the pageant, which then derives additional income from ticket sales. These scam operations are nearly always multilevel, beginning at the community level and proceeding to the world competition. The promoters make money at *all* levels.
6. The most despicable is saved for last. Here the "talent agency" generally preys upon young men and women who are signed to a contract and then transported across the country where they are forced into prostitution and other activities. They are frequently virtually prisoners and have no one to whom they feel they can turn for assistance.

When dealing with any talent or modeling agency or any pageant or other promotion, carefully check on the business before entering into any arrangements. Be especially leery of relatively new operations or of any operation where anything seems even slightly out of the ordinary.

5

Charity Rackets and Frauds on the Sick or Elderly (Swindlers Have No Heart)

CHARITY RACKETS

It is a sad commentary on human nature that the generosity of Americans in trying to help those in need and in trying to eliminate some of society's greatest problems is constantly and profitably exploited by operators of dishonest charity rackets. Millions of dollars each year, intended by the donors to further charitable causes, are diverted into the pockets of these swindlers. For the most part, the secret of their success is to imitate the techniques employed by legitimate charities and rely on the fact that those solicited will not take the time or effort necessary to tell the difference. Fraudulent charity schemes range from unsophisticated door-to-door solicitations to highly sophisticated appeals to major corporate contributors.

The doorbell rings and it's a moderately poverty-stricken looking young person soliciting funds for Canines with Muscular Dystrophy or some other charity that is not readily recognizable to you. If you give him a chance he'll relate a well-rehearsed sob story that you'll find hard to resist. Somewhere in the neighborhood is the young person's "supervisor," who provides transportation, makes area assignments and gives pep talks to the youngsters working on a minimal commission basis. Chances are you'll give the kid a few quarters just to get rid of him or because he's managed to make you feel embarrassed if you don't give him something. If you do give anything, you'll be giving the money for the support of swindlers.

A door-to-door solicitor for phony charities may even offer to send you a "token of appreciation" in exchange for your generosity.

The more substantial the "token" the more suspicious you should be. You'll probably never see it.

Street corner beggars are frequently talented amateur psychologists. In a large city they can earn up to $15,000.00 per year by mastering certain psychological techniques for getting people to part with very small amounts of money. And remember that no one is withholding taxes on that amount. In one documented account a summertime street corner beggar in New York spent his winters at his condominium on the Florida coast.

Telephone solicitors for phony charities can be particularly effective in imitating a legitimate charity. The caller says he is calling on behalf of a local charity you may or may not have heard of, and he's selling tickets to a circus, sporting event or other entertainment event. You hate to say no because the cause sounds like a worthy one. So you let the caller put a couple of tickets in the mail and you pay for them when they arrive the next day — still not knowing whether the solicitation is legitimate.

Even if the solicitation is legitimate in the sense that a charity is actually involved and an actual fund-raising event will take place, the caller may not tell the whole story. He may not reveal, for example, that only 10 percent of the net proceeds are actually going to the charity. The other 90 percent goes to the professional promoters. Some state laws now require that either the majority of the proceeds go to charity or the precise breakdown must be disclosed to persons solicited. You should always attempt to determine the amount of promotional fees that are paid to professional fund raisers.

Charity fraud through the mails does occur, but it tends to be less effective than person-to-person or telephone contacts because of the lack of a high-pressure pitch from a fast talker and because of the availability of time to investigate and evaluate the solicitation.

Because businesses are anxious to generate goodwill and are sometimes concerned about their social responsibilities, they are frequently vulnerable to charity frauds. One such scheme involved mail, telephone and person-to-person solicitation of businesses by persons alleging an affiliation with a nonprofit minority group organization. In exchange for a contribution the business would be listed in a national magazine distributed by the minority organization. The businessmen are not informed that the alleged charitable organization doesn't have any goals other than the support of those involved and the magazine is distributed, if at all, to only a handful of people.

Businessmen are also well advised to seek to determine whether administrative expenses in a charitable solicitation might be excessive. A local charity may lend its name to the promotion of an entertainment event in return for a very small percentage of the take. Businesses that believe that they are contributing to the charity by buying blocks of tickets have a right to know that 90 percent of the proceeds are going to the promoters.

How do you avoid becoming the victim of charity fraud? Let's start with a few basics. The burden should always be on the solicitor to prove the legitimacy of his cause. After all, you're the one being asked to part with your hard-earned money, not him. Don't presume that it isn't a fraud. Make him identify himself completely and supply all the information you ask for. If you don't really like the cause or you're not convinced it's legitimate *don't give*. Don't let the solicitor make you feel embarrassed not to give. Politely tell him you're not interested.

High-pressure tactics should result in a flat refusal to give. You should be given time to investigate as much as you want. Legitimate charities don't operate on a "last chance to give" basis. Be suspicious of any charity you have not heard of and that does not have a permanent office in your locality. A telephone solicitation followed by immediate pickup of a donation in person is the first sign of a fly-by-night operation.

Never fall for the line that the charity does not take checks in order to hold down administrative costs. All legitimate charities take checks. The only reasons not to take a check are to avoid making a stop at the bank on the way out of town and to avoid leaving behind a paper trail of any kind.

Both individuals and businesses might want to insist that any charity they contribute to has previously been approved for deductions by an Internal Revenue Service ruling. Also they should not be afraid to demand a certified financial statement before giving.

There are plenty of worthy causes around that deserve the support of charitable givers. It is therefore inexcusable for society to tolerate the waste of charitable dollars caused by fraudulent schemes. Law enforcement can and should educate the public and investigate and prosecute vigorously the offenders. But each citizen also has a responsibility to make sure his carelessness doesn't contribute to the problem.

LONELY HEARTS CLUBS

Loneliness is a powerful emotion upon which the unscrupulous prey, sometimes with devastating results.

A common ploy is the so-called lonely hearts club, which offers a type of matchmaking service for a fee. Such clubs may be legitimate social clubs that have social interaction as a prime purpose. Unfortunately, the field has historically been dominated by several varieties of fraud.

The least harmful type is the club that procures someone else's name for you — a pen pal — for an exorbitant fee. Far more dangerous are the lonely hearts clubs that are "fronts" for con men bent on extortion, theft or even murder. No character references are required before placing an advertisement for providing this type of service. By responding (usually to a box number) you may literally be placing your life in the hands of a maniac. There are not many recorded cases of such a club being established solely for the purpose of murder. But there are more than a few instances in which murder later came into the picture as a means of obtaining insurance benefits or becoming heir to an estate.

Professional con men will either run the clubs or use them to obtain names. They are aware that many of the people who enroll are older persons who are financially well off but lonely. These people become prime targets. The con man will relieve them of as much money as possible through various schemes. In fact, lonely hearts clubs have frequently been utilized as the primary source of victims for confidence games and pigeon drops.

The swindlers are not above entering into a marriage to accomplish their goals if the rewards appear substantial enough. Since an abundance of patience is not one of the virtues these individuals possess they may arrange an "accident" to become heir to the estate or to collect on the double indemnity policy taken out shortly after the marriage.

There is no question that these bizarre types of occurrences are not the norm. But the risk is always present and it is very difficult to (1) properly screen the club itself and (2) screen club referrals to you, which the clubs normally perform in a very perfunctory manner.

A variation of the lonely hearts club is the computer dating service. Few of these services have large numbers of members and screening is again generally perfunctory. The computer allegedly is matching people on the basis of information supplied by the individual. Again there is generally no other background check made.

Another problem is that the computer dating service may consider your area to be a geographical region and submit potential dates to you who reside several hundred miles away. That's acceptable if you don't mind cross-country dating. If that is not appealing check with the service to find out exactly how many persons in your city or county are members.

Remember that the services performed by lonely hearts clubs and dating services have inherent risks. The same objective, meeting other people, can be accomplished free through churches, political clubs and other legitimate organizations. Becoming acquainted may be an alternative motive in such settings but alternative motives presented in a lonely hearts club setting can be much more devious and much more costly.

MEDICAL FRAUDS

The patient walked into a darkened room and removed the hospital gown. She stood, nude, with her hands pointing to the north as different-colored lights played on her breasts. After several minutes had elapsed the lights went out and she donned the robe and went into the outer office. It was the eighth time she had undergone this treatment, at a cost of $25.00 per treatment. During the weeks she had undergone treatment, the lump in her right breast had continued to grow. She was repeatedly assured this was "part of the cure."

A person in such a position may eventually seek legitimate medical care. But the wasted time could result in radical surgery or even death. There are hundreds of such quack cures foisted upon an ignorant and sometimes desperate public. At best they delay a person from seeking necessary help. At worst they prey upon desperate people who have terminal illnesses with the only result being that the victim divests himself of large sums of money before dying.

Medical frauds range from the diet pills that produce no results up to and including fake cancer cures and fake cures for arthritic conditions. These frauds are made easier by the rapid advances in medical science. Miracle cures are not inconceivable. Thus even the most outlandish of claims has about it a patina of believability.

Consider the company that advertises weight loss. It promises huge weight reduction if one will but use the pills and potions purveyed to the purchaser. And it matters not, say the advertisements, how much one eats. The more one consumes the more weight he will lose on this magical medical plan. Preposterous. But the "guaranteed results" draw thousands of orders and the company makes nearly a quarter of a million before it can be shut down.

Move up the scale in desperation. Consider the young mother who is confined to a wheelchair because of rheumatoid arthritis. She is in constant pain and desperate for any conceivable form of relief. There is a quack willing to assist her. He may foist a copper bracelet upon her at a cost of $5.00 or he may begin an involved treatment procedure with a machine he has just invented. He carefully explains that the treatment is experimental in nature and he cannot guarantee results. But he is quick to discuss the several dozen people who were in worse shape than the young mother, all of whom made miraculous progress. One of them, in fact, just returned to work in a factory after having been a bed patient for four years. Cost of treatment? $100.00 per session. The sessions can be scheduled nearly forever. And when the machine is disassembled it is found to contain a series of blinking lights and a small electric motor that produces a curious humming noise. It has no medical value whatsoever.

Take one more step up the ladder of desperation. We find here a middle-aged executive who has been told he has inoperable cancer and has only six months to live. He is searching for any reprieve, and not only a reprieve but a long life is offered by the seller of a magnetic machine that produces the faintest hint of an electrical shock. The machine sells for $1,200.00 and can be used in the home. It forestalls death not one whit.

Name the disease: senility, loss of hearing, diabetes or acne. It has a fraudulent cure somewhere. All age levels are targets but some are more susceptible than others. Consider the elderly person who lives alone, has no relatives and is approaching senility. Smooth-talking medical quacks are quick to separate these people from their life savings.

There are those who profit from the pain of others. There are mechanical monsters that offer no legitimate aid. And there are hundreds of dietary supplements that will cure any problem the body may have or prevent any potential problems before they occur. Thousands of items are sold through the mails. All of these frauds do have one thing in common — the victim must in some way assent to the purchase or use of the "product."

That is not the case with elderly or disabled persons who are confined in substandard nursing homes where the costs are extremely high in comparison to the care given. Medical treatments for which charges are made may not have been performed. Meals may frequently not be served. And who is to complain? Consider the alternatives for an elderly bedridden patient who has no relatives and whose bills are paid by public assistance benefits. Such patients are warehoused awaiting death. The only reason their life matters to the nursing home is because upon death the money supply dries up.

Or consider those who have some means and are capable of caring for themselves. They may opt for a life care center, which is available only to those 65 and above. For several thousand dollars minimum and certain monthly assessments, these people receive care for life. Have you checked the insurance tables for projected longevity past the age of 65? You will find that on an average the life care center will be well compensated for its care. And that's assuming the center is legitimate and does not later teeter over the brink into bankruptcy, resulting in the displacement of all the residents who now no longer have independent resources.

What all this proves is that man's capacity for inhumanity to his fellowman, especially when money is involved, is beyond measure. And it is an especially difficult area to deal with because nearly every fraud or despicable living situation mentioned has a very legitimate counterpart where cures are sought, where living conditions are excellent and where the humanity displayed is also beyond measure. In addition, the desperation of the victims makes it unlikely that they will be the ones to report frauds if they have the capability to do so.

The only sure defenses against such preparations are an abundance of caution and the willingness to check on extravagant claims before expending money. The small number of con men who prey upon the ill and the elderly have no scruples. They will claim anything in order to sell their product.

Avoidance is the prescription, one not always easy to follow.

RELIGIOUS FRAUDS

Talking about fraud and religion in the same breath is an invitation to controversy. Some people's sensitivities will no doubt be offended when the motivations of a religious person or organization are called into question. They correctly point out that the mere fact that a religious activity seems to be accompanied by an almost "miraculous" ability to raise and spend money does not necessarily make the religious effort an insincere one. The simple fact seems to be that one man's religion is another man's fraud and vice versa.

With that caveat it is nevertheless necessary to point out that the trappings of religion have provided many a rogue with the wherewithal to separate well-intentioned believers from their hard-earned money. Some of America's most famous big-time swindlers have exploited their mastery of biblical passages to accomplish unholy deeds. Religious fraud is therefore a topic that merits discussion in any consideration of significant fraudulent schemes.

Almost without exception fraud has been able to infiltrate religion only in those instances in which religion and business become inextricably combined. The most notable religion-oriented scams perpetrated in recent times have each involved the issuance of stocks, bonds or promissory notes. The avowed purpose of such instruments, of course, is to finance the Lord's work. But in the hands of the wrong people the Lord's work may be indistinguishable from the work of the devil. Such was the case when a few ministers turned con men started the Baptist Foundation of America. The Baptist Foundation of America held itself out in an impressive array of literature as "a monument to faith in God and to freedom and courage of the human spirit." Its mission to serve God by helping mankind was to include everything from hospitals to a retirement home for ministers. With prominent ministers as its hierarchy the Baptist Foundation of America quickly acquired an aura of religious respectability. Numerous swindlers were allowed to make donations of relatively worthless assets and take huge tax deductions in return. With a highly inflated balance sheet the foundation set about acquiring subsidiaries that would supposedly assist in doing the Lord's work. This was done through the issuance of $26 million in notes to the public. The public was convinced of the soundness of their investment not only because of the involvement of men of the cloth but also the use of falsified financial statements. A clean bill of health from Dun and Bradstreet didn't hurt either. The Baptist Foundation of America's notes were accepted as collateral by some of America's most respected lending institutions. But the notes were worth less than the paper they were written on. Most of the major religious frauds of the past quarter century have been accomplished in a similar fashion.

As long as the financial side of religion involves only the support of the minister and the maintenance of the church facility the opportunities for the perpetration of fraud are limited. But when the financial interests of the church become complex and diverse the members of the congregation should not consider it sinful to proceed cautiously. If the minister proposing expansion of financial interests is new on the scene make sure his credentials don't include a criminal rap sheet.

6

Commercial Fraud Schemes (Getting "The Business")

ADVANCE LOAN FEE SCHEMES

> MONEY TO LEND
> Up to $25,000 and more available on nonsecured basis to credit worthy individuals. Contact Mr. James, Room 222, Home Motel, between 2 and 4 P.M., Fri. and Sat.

Samuel T. Smith has owned his business for five years. He has made modest profits but feels they could be substantially larger if he had sufficient capital for expansion. Mr. Smith has a line of credit with his local bank but is not in a position where the bank will lend him sufficient funds to allow him to enlarge and remodel his facility.

The above advertisement appeared in the Sunday edition of the local newspaper. It happened to catch Sam Smith's eye. He telephoned Mr. James and made an appointment to see him. Sam appeared at the scheduled time and introduced himself to Mr. James, who turned out to be a very likeable fellow. During the next hour Mr. James and Mr. Smith formed a budding friendship.

"Sam, I think we're going to be able to do business. I think we'll really be good for each other's business."

During the next half hour Sam and Mr. James computed the amount of money necessary for the planned expansion. They determined the cost of remodeling at $55,000.00 and figured Sam would reasonably need five years to repay the loan. "Tell you what, Sam, let's fill out the necessary papers and then we'll go down to the lounge and have a drink to celebrate." There followed a quick examination of a sheaf of papers. At the bottom of each Sam dutifully signed his name. "Great, Sam. Now your check for $2,000.00 and we'll be finished." Sam was slightly taken aback. He hadn't heard anything up to this point about his paying Mr. James.

"I'm borrowing the money, what in the world is the $2,000.00 for?"

Mr. James apologized.

"I'm sorry, Sam. I guess I didn't explain this document here. We were so busy talking that I neglected to tend to business. The $2,000.00 is broken down with $1,600.00 as advance interest payments. You get credit for that during the term of the loan. The $400.00 remaining is a processing fee, which is a one-time-only payment. You realize that, as much as I have grown to trust you personally, this lending is a risky business. That's why we require the advance fees. It gives debtors an added incentive to pay back the loan as they already have a stake in the outcome." That seemed logical enough to Sam. He paid the money, went down to the lounge for a drink (which Mr. James bought) and went home with the promise that the $55,000.00 loan would close within 30 days.

Eight days later Sam received a telephone call. "Sam, I'm calling about your loan." Seems that the parent company was willing to make the loan but not at the rate of interest quoted by Mr. James. "It will require an additional $450.00 advance interest from you. After that check clears I'll put the loan proceeds in the mail." To make the transaction simpler, Mr. James suggested a certified check so the loan proceeds could be sent by return mail. Sam hesitated. But he had already invested $2,000.00. And he did need the loan. So he sent the certified check. And he waited. And he waited. And he waited. Sam tried everything. The telephone number was disconnected. The address was a vacant lot in Chicago. And Mr. James was not to be found.

Said Sam six months later, "I never even learned his first name."

Potential borrowers attempting to identify fraudulent lenders should look for certain warning signs.

1. Legitimate lenders will always closely scrutinize the venture for which a loan is requested, whereas advance fee operators typically pay little attention to the risk involved (because for them there is none) and merely flatter the borrower about the worthiness of his proposed undertaking.

2. The fraudulent loan operator will discourage the borrower from taking the time and effort to check him out thoroughly and will discourage him from having an attorney review the transaction. Never rely on the lender's list of references unless it includes persons and institutions you know as reliable.
3. If "good faith" is cited as the reason for collecting an advance fee, you are probably not dealing with a legitimate lender.
4. Do not meet lenders at hotels or airports for the purpose of finalizing loans and paying advance loan fees.
5. If advance fees are proposed insist that they be placed in escrow with an attorney or institution you trust. Legitimate lenders do not need advance fees to "live off of" and will gladly accept payment of the fees when the loan is finally closed.

BUST-OUTS AND BANKRUPTCY FRAUDS

Bankruptcy fraud essentially involves the purchase of merchandise on credit, disposal of the goods for cash, concealment of the proceeds and finally filing for bankruptcy.

Bankruptcy fraud may also be called planned bankruptcy or bust-out. But probably more correctly defined a bust-out is a bankruptcy fraud sans filing of bankruptcy. It has been estimated that such frauds are responsible for losses of from $80 to $100 million annually. Bankruptcy fraud can easily destroy smaller businesses that sell goods to the fradulent business on credit.

Those who perpetrate bankruptcy frauds usually fall into one of three main categories:

1. Those who are members of organized criminal groups.
2. Those classified as "con men" who are not members of any organized group.
3. Previously legitimate businessmen who turn to fraud in an attempt to salvage something from the ashes of their failing businesses.

In that third category, consider Gem-K, a medium-sized manufacturing concern that has been in business for just over a year. For the past few months the business has sunk deeper and deeper into the financial swamp of insolvency as the partners have poured all their individual assets into the venture. With the specter of bankruptcy looming larger, the partners begin groping for a way out — any way out. After obtaining expert financial advice from their bartender, the partners change Gem-K's methods of doing business. During the next few weeks material that is ordered is diverted into a rental warehouse on the south side of the city. Orders remain unfilled and as soon as the partners have exhausted all remaining sources of credit they file for bankruptcy. The ploy is perfectly legitimate except for their "neglect" to show the items in the warehouse as assets. The partners have diverted assets in anticipation of insolvency so that these assets cannot later be sold by the trustee in bankruptcy to benefit creditors.

Thus, much as necessity is said to be the mother of invention, desperation gives birth to the involvement of the partners in crime. There are numerous variations of the scheme. Another twist involves a planned bankruptcy in which the criminal intent is present from the inception.

In this scenario consider the ACD Corporation, which is a medium-sized distributing firm that has been in business for fifteen years, has annual gross sales of $2.2 million and makes a net profit of approximately $220,000.00 annually. The corporation holds real estate valued at $5.7 million and has additional assets of $1.4 million as well as an inventory valued at approximately $600,000.00.

In January following an internal fight over stock sales, three new directors were named to the five-man board. One of the three was named general manager, supplanting the corporate executive who had held the post for the past twelve years. During the past ten months, the assets of the corporation have been sold for cash. A 90-percent mortgage was taken out on the real estate, which had been free and clear. The corporation previously had paid for all orders as they came due. It now purchases on credit and allows the bills to become 30-, then 60- and finally 90-day overdue accounts. Needless to say, as soon as the corporation has been milked for all it's worth and the cash transferred to a nice Swiss bank account, the directors vote to file for bankruptcy, leaving a previously profitable corporation owing substantially more than it can pay. The corporation ceases operation and the three directors move on to their next assignment.

With either type of bankruptcy fraud there can be numerous sidelines including planned thefts and fencing activities with the stolen merchandise channeled through the corporation for conversion to cash. In the event bankruptcy is filed it is "explained" by blaming it on a theft, on a fire that destroyed a warehouse (on which high insurance claims are filed), on a "messy divorce," on alcohol or gambling problems, etc., etc., *ad nauseam*.

Another planned bust-out scam is the establishment of a company that has a name (and perhaps an address) very similar to a nationally recognized concern that has top credit ratings. The scam firm then orders easily disposable merchandise from unrelated firms with the intent of converting it to cash and then closing the scam operation, which is usually merely an answering service. Because the perpetrators of a bust-out don't take the time to file bankruptcy their operation is usually an extremely mobile one. They spend no more than a few months in each town, buying as many readily transportable goods as possible on credit. They move out quickly and suddenly, taking the goods with them to be disposed of in another town.

There are numerous subtle tip-offs that may indicate a bankruptcy or bust-out scam is in progress. They may be summed up by advising businesses to beware of major changes in personnel, ordering and payment patterns, especially when several of these changes occur at the same time. Recheck the firm's credit ratings, insisting upon updated materials including independently audited statements. The extra measures may not be sufficient to prevent the scam from being completed but they may be enough to keep an individual from becoming a creditor of the crooked firm. That result is worth the extra trouble.

CHECK FRAUD SCHEMES

Check fraud (or "hanging bad paper" as it's known in the criminal vernacular) takes many forms. Most bad checks are passed by amateurs who are motivated by their own financial problems or their impulsive desire to beat the system. However, many sophisticated check frauds are perpetrated by professional criminals acting out a well-planned scenario. While even the elaborate schemes are too numerous to mention, the mention of a few will serve to demonstrate their basic *modus operandi*.

A check passer opens an account with an initial cash deposit and receives a stamped duplicate of the deposit slip. The same day he approaches several different tellers at the same bank, each time cashing checks by showing the deposit slip to prove he has funds to cover it. His goal is to cash checks with a total sum far in excess of the initial deposit.

A person purporting to be a local corporate executive calls a small bank and indicates his assistant will arrive shortly to transact some business and requests the assistant be instructed to call him. The assistant arrives, receives the message and calls. Having thus established a false identity he talks the bank into cashing his counterfeit check bearing the name of the local company.

A check ring may form a bogus company and acquire payroll checks. In a matter of days "employees" will cash them with local merchants, who when they call the company are assured the check is genuine. The operation is quick and profitable.

One of the most common schemes involves using worthless checks to open accounts or purchase merchandise, always presenting a check in excess of the intended deposit or in excess of the purchase and asking for the balance in cash. In this manner a ring of check passers can accumulate large amounts of cash in a short time and be on their way to new towns with new victims.

There is a variety of warning signals that might properly lead someone to suspect check fraud is in the offing. Here are just a few. The handwriting of the person presenting a check may be out of character with his age and status in life. The check writer may write his signature suspiciously slowly. The type on a counterfeit check may contain misspelled names and addresses or the payee's name on the endorsement may be spelled differently than on the face of the check. Oddly shaped numerals may indicate the check has been tampered with as would poor spacing, erasures, or changes in ink colors or line thicknesses. A person who is an overly glib or distracting talker, or who tries to rush the check cashing process because "he's late for an appointment," may be just a con artist trying to hang bad paper. If a juvenile presents a government pension check for cashing (the purpose for which the check is issued is indicated on the left side of government checks), something is seriously wrong.

The requirement of adequate identification from a check passer cannot be overemphasized. Photos on identification cards should be closely checked against the appearance of the check casher and the address of the customer on an identifying document should be checked against the address on a personal check he attempts to cash.

Symptoms of possible fraud in connection with the use of stolen or counterfeit traveler's checks include the cashing of many traveler's checks at one time, the countersigning of traveler's checks in advance, the purchase of low-priced items with high-denomination checks and the use of the check casher's free hand to obstruct the cashier's view of the countersigning of the checks.

For the true professional or the talented amateur "check kiting" can be among the most sophisticated and most profitable of fraudulent schemes. Kiting is the illegal manipulation of funds between two or more banks where the kiter takes advantage of the time lag in the check collection process, often referred to as the float. When a person cashes a check at one bank, drawn on another bank, the check will not physically reach the other bank for an average of one to five days, depending upon the geographic proximity of the banks.

A kite scheme will typically start with the kiter opening a checking account in a bank in city A using a $250.00 check drawn on a bank in city B as an initial deposit. Assume this happens on January 1. The deposit check is drawn on nonexistent funds. The following day the kiter or his accomplice deposits a check for $300.00 in the bank in city B drawn on the bank in city A. This is to cover the check that the city A bank is forwarding to the city B bank for payment. On January 3, the kiter deposits at the city A bank a check for $400.00 drawn on the city B bank. On January 4, the kiter returns to the bank in city B and makes a $500.00 deposit drawn on the bank in city A.

In four days the total of nonexistent funds deposited at both banks is $1,450.00. On the morning of January 5 the banks' checking account journals will reflect balances of $350.00 and $550.00 respectively. The kiter will proceed to withdraw these funds, in cash, and leave for greener pastures with his $900.00 profit.

The telltale signs of a check kiting scheme include deposits of steadily increasing amounts on a frequent basis, frequent withdrawals payable to the same person, deposit items drawn on like name accounts at other banks and frequent depositer requests to check the account balance.

There is one extremely effective tool that banks can utilize to deter check kiting. If a kiting scheme is suspected a single uncollected funds hold on a questionable deposit will quickly flush out the scheme and prevent a substantial financial loss.

COMPUTER CRIMES

Depending upon their orientation in life most people either view computers as the greatest of modern inventions or as a diabolical force that will eventually conquer the world and make slaves of humanity. Regardless of who's right and who's wrong the proliferation of computers in our society is undeniable. One can readily foresee that computers will literally be a household item. One area in which computers are already extremely useful is in financial matters of considerable volume and complexity. For example, many payrolls in both the governmental and private sector are met through the use of computers. And where there is money there is crime. Because of the inability of most people to understand computer processes, business has never been more vulnerable to crime.

The use of computers to steal money, bonds or negotiable instruments is a criminal act that is already significant, but one that has by no means reached its potential. One stumbling block to an accurate determination of the extent of the computer crime problem is that computer crimes are generally thought to be grossly underreported. Nothing is more embarrassing for an organization than to admit that employees are stealing them blind because of their inability to control their own technology. Even when reported, computer crime is the most complex of economic crimes and investigation and prosecution is sometimes hampered by this complexity.

There appears to be no limit to the ways in which a creative crook can use a computer as an aid in the perpetration of complex financial swindles. This fact was dramatically illustrated in the case of the

Equity Funding Corporation of America, which many in law enforcement have labeled "the fraud of the century." False data were fed into a computer to mislead the financial world concerning the financial condition of the corporation. Officers of Equity Funding created fake insurance policies, which were recorded in the company's computer system and sold to other insurance companies. The fake policies in the computer were corroborated by fake medical and credit files. Over $2 billion in money and other assets was manipulated in this manner.

Embezzlement by computer also has unlimited potential. One well-known scheme involves bank tellers using a computer to transfer interest payments away from customers and into their own accounts.

Computers have been used to steal various kinds of property. A computer was used to steal 200 freight cars from a large railroad. A man used a computer to steal $1 million worth of equipment by having a corporate computer place orders for equipment and then have it delivered to him.

Thefts of computer data are a significant aspect of industrial espionage operations. Even more frequently, employees have illegally profited by selling confidential programs and customer lists to competitors.

One of the common forms of computer crime, and perhaps the most costly to organizations that are victims, is that which involves employees using expensive computer time without the knowledge of the employer. To resolve ambiguities in existing statutes some states are passing specific computer crime statutes that expressly make theft of computer time a criminal offense.

The computer criminal may be motivated in a traditional manner, by greed, or he may be a complex personality who sees the computer as a symbol of the establishment and his crime as a victimless one. Or perhaps he is motivated, at least in part, by the intellectual challenge. The fact that computer crimes typically involve greater economic benefits than other crimes and yet are still hard to detect may also be a factor in the decision to commit a computer crime. Computer crime statistics complied thus far have produced a profile of the typical computer abuser. Usually a male, he is an amateur criminal with no previous record. He is young and very intelligent and may well be disgruntled concerning treatment by his employer.

There are indications that organized crime has discovered the profits available in computer crime and considers it a new frontier for criminal exploitation.

Experts indicate that the vulnerability of a computer system to fraud is increased by the presence of some or all of the following factors:

1. The computer generates negotiable instruments or is used to transfer credit, process loans or obtain credit ratings.

2. Access to computer facilities is not limited to those with the need to know.
3. Separation of key computer functions is inadequate either in terms of responsibility or of physical proximity.
4. Use of computers after regular hours or during night shifts is loosely supervised.
5. Auditors do not have sufficient knowledge of computer operations to include the computer system in their audits.
6. Key computer operators are only subject to routine screening by the personnel department.

Computer fraud may first come to the attention of management when computer generated data seem inconsistent with their notions of how the business is progressing. Or it may be discovered that confidential computer data are somehow getting out of the plant. Or employees might begin to complain about paycheck irregularities. Or a customer complains about billing irregularities. In fact consumers who take the time to complain about a seemingly insignificant billing error may lead to the detection of computer fraud.

Insofar as computer system security is involved, the computer processing department should be separate. Functions and authority should be separate with no employee having control over an entire operation. Inventories should be kept of computer data. Passwords and keys should be changed periodically. The security system itself should be frequently audited, analyzed and improved.

In conclusion, consumers who want to prepare themselves for the computer age ahead will do well to become educated concerning computers to an extent that they will view them as something other than just "magic boxes." Part of that education is recognizing that computers are and will remain a potential instrumentality of crime.

CONSTRUCTION FRAUD

In recent years scandals involving large construction projects have been uncovered with alarming regularity. Often the government, and hence the taxpaying public, has been the victim. Scandals have involved bid rigging, fraudulent acquisition of performance bonds, phony or inflated subcontracts, use of inferior materials and a host of other abuses. Frequently, elements of organized crime have been involved.

But fraud is not exclusive to large-scale construction projects. Even the little guy must be wary to protect himself against fraud in the construction of his home or business and when undertaking remodeling or improvement projects. Unfortunately it is all too easy to call oneself a contractor and many people represent themselves as contractors without having the skills or financial backing to deserve this status.

The consumer who undertakes a construction project can find his greatest protection in observing four basic steps. Step one dictates that no construction contract be signed unless and until clear and detailed plans and specifications have been prepared by a reputable contractor or architectural firm. Step two is to solicit bids from several local contractors based on the plans and specifications. Know each contractor who is asked to submit a bid. Investigate his credentials, his reputation and his compliance with local licensing regulations. Talk to other people he's done work for. And remember, hiring the lowest bidder is not necessarily the best deal. Step three is to have the construction contract and other pertinent documents reviewed by an attorney. Step four is to completely arrange financing of the project before the construction contract is signed. Following these steps drastically reduces the chances of being victimized by a dishonest contractor.

The fraudulent contractor can create problems with far-reaching implications. The lien laws in most states provide that if a contractor fails to pay laborers, suppliers or subcontractors, these persons can put a lien on the real estate involved. Thus the owner of the property could pay the contractor in full and if the contractor then fails to meet his obligations to subcontractors or suppliers the owner could wind up paying double just to get the liens removed. As long as the liens remain on the property it cannot be sold or further mortgaged. Means of avoiding double payment include guarantee bonds, holding funds in escrow until potential lien holders are paid or joining the subcontractor or materialman as a payee on every check issued by the property owner. Subcontractors and suppliers who have been paid should be required to sign lien waivers. If nothing else, a system of payment should be set up whereby the contractor must submit lien waivers before substantial payments are released to him. Many states have begun to enact criminal statutes providing penalties for contractors who cause liens to be filed against property by willfully failing to pay subcontractors or suppliers. In fact the general thrust of legislation in this area is toward greater protection of the property owner.

Another common abuse in the construction field involves the contractor convincing the property owner to sign a completion certificate prior to actual completion of the job. A completion certificate states the job has been completed to your satisfaction and in accordance with plans and specifications. Signing it prematurely may allow the contractor to get full payment before the job is done and gives you little recourse if the remaining work is not completed satisfactorily.

Never allow a contractor to tell you that it is not necessary to put an aspect of an agreement in writing because "you have his word on it." Such verbal assertions will be of no avail if and when a dispute leads to litigation. Certain matters should always be covered in the contract. It should require strict adherence to the plans and specifications. A completion date should be set with sanctions for noncompliance. The contract should contain warranties with respect to materials and workmanship. The contractor should supply written assurances of his compliance with various legal requirements and that he is adequately insured to assume the risks of the project. Further, a contract should require that changes in the contract can occur only when both parties sign a written change order.

With respect to some of the fraudulent schemes discussed in this book the ability of the individual to protect himself is limited by the presence of factors outside his control. Not so with respect to construction frauds. The diligence of a consumer in attempting to protect himself from construction fraud will almost always result in a proportional minimization of the risks.

CORPORATE SHELL GAMES

A shell is a corporation without substantial assets. It is usually a company that has gone broke and become dormant without calling in its stock or taking the formal steps to dissolve. If the company has been through a Securities and Exchange Commission registration so that its stock can be sold publicly, the shell itself may remain a marketable asset. By acquiring such a company, changing its name and installing some figureheads without criminal records as corporate officers, stock fraud artists are ready to prey on an unsuspecting public. The misuse of corporate shells has been an essential ingredient in many million-dollar swindles.

The first task of those who take over a shell corporation is to reduce the old shareholders' equity. This can be done by declaring a reverse stock split. For example, old shareholders may be given one share for each hundred shares they used to own. The swindlers then find themselves a broker-dealer to act as a "market maker" for a new issue of corporate stock. Trading is always done on over-the-counter markets and current prices are followed in a daily quotation service. The market maker has a supply of stock on hand and frequently tries to push the stock on his customers. The whole process can have a snowballing effect with worthless stock selling for a continuing rising price. The fraud is completed when the manipulators manage to pass off the worthless stock as collateral for loans or in exchange for genuine assets.

In the past, favorite corporate shells have been connected with data processing, mining and minerals, land development and dog racing tracks. A typical shell game was the case of Texas Uranium Corporation. Texas Uranium went broke in 1957 after a brief three-year existence. Ten years later it was acquired specifically for the perpetration of a shell game because it still held legal authority to issue five million shares of stock. Within no time the company made certain "acquisitions" and assigned arbitrary values to them. The corporate balance sheet soon reflected assets of almost $5 million. By the time the Securities and Exchange Commission halted trading in Texas Uranium in 1968 the masterminds behind it had managed to sell their shares for considerable sums. All shell games involve similar scenarios.

When you are approached concerning acquisition of stock that is being pushed by a brokerage firm acting as a market maker, or are asked to take stock in an obscure company as part of a business transaction, it is wise to do some research regarding the history of the corporation. It may prevent you from becoming a pawn in a corporate shell game.

COUPON FRAUD

As insidious as it may seem, even those "10¢ off" coupons you cut from your local newspaper are a vehicle for criminal abuse.

A coupon is a written offer of a cash discount or free product, issued by the manufacturer of the product to prospective purchasers and redeemable by the retailer who sells the product. The coupon contains the terms of the offer and promises retailers that the manufacturer will reimburse the retailer for its face value.

Most retailers who accept coupons will forward them to a clearinghouse rather than directly to the manufacturer. The clearinghouse sorts, counts and invoices the coupons and pays the retailer for the total amount of coupons received. The clearinghouse then ships the coupons to the various manufacturers, who pay the clearinghouse the face value of the coupons plus a handling charge for its services.

The coupon business is a big one. Coupon redemption involves hundreds of millions of dollars each year. Thus it constitutes an invitation to the criminal element of our society to exploit yet another opportunity for fraud.

Fraudulent "misredemption" takes on several forms. Mail carriers may fail to deliver direct mail coupons and sell them elsewhere for fraudulent redemption. Newspaper personnel may sell unused coupon inserts at a reduced rate for fraudulent redemption. Retailers may submit coupons that do not represent corresponding purchases. Coupon clearinghouses may "pad" legitimate retail coupon shipments or submit coupons under fictitious store names. Finally, organized criminal elements may procure or counterfeit large quantities of coupons and submit them to fictitious retail outlets or sell them to unethical retailers or clearinghouses.

Admittedly many of these schemes, by their very nature, will not be susceptible to detection by the average consumer. But if you should become aware that someone is counterfeiting coupons or is offering to sell coupons at a discount you can be sure that fraud is afoot. Don't let anyone try to tell you that it is a regular course of business to sell coupons to another person at a discount price. That's simply not true. By not becoming involved you may save yourself some problems. By reporting such scams you may save all shoppers some money.

A scheme that is all too familiar to many consumers is the sale of a book of coupons from local merchants offering discounts on various products and services. In a typical example, the promoter tells you that the book, which sells for $10.00, contains $500.00 worth of products and services.

Most purchasers of such "bargains" are eventually disappointed. Usually, it's simply a matter of the book being a lousy investment. The products or services are not very desirable and the time period for the use of coupons is too restrictive. But fraud has also plagued the coupon book business.

If the promoter is a boiler room operator, he may print coupons without the authorization of the merchants, conduct an intensive short term telephone solicitation, and then move on, leaving an embarrassed consumer trying to pass off a phony coupon on an equally embarrassed merchant. Or money may be collected and coupon books never delivered. More often than not, a charitable or civic organization is enticed into the operation to enhance its appeal. The organization gets a percentage of the gross sales in return for the use of its name. Whatever its name, if the organization is not careful to verify the legitimacy of the promoter, its name will be mud when the promoter is gone and the complaints start rolling in from consumers and merchants alike.

Another problem with such coupon books has been deceit on the part of the participating merchants. One such incident involved an auto repair garage that authorized a coupon for a brake overhaul at a greatly reduced price. The coupon instructed the consumer to make an appointment for the brake overhaul by calling the garage and asking for Joe. The offer was good between July 1st and October 1st. Anyone who called and asked for Joe and then tried to make an appointment was told that the garage was booked for brake work until November. If you called and didn't ask for Joe, or didn't otherwise reveal that you had a coupon, you could get an appointment for the next day.

If you have a compulsion to buy a coupon book, by all means thoroughly investigate the nature of the promotion and the bargains that are available. Remember, a coupon for free snow removal which is good between June 1st and September 1st may not be as valuable as they want you to believe.

CREDIT CAPERS

It used to be that extensions of credit were a frequent source of fraud and of financial loss to consumers. But legislation, primarily the "truth in lending" law, has greatly reduced the extent of fraud in credit transactions. Unfortunately, the loss to consumers from inadvisable credit transactions remains high, for the simple reason that the public remains poorly educated concerning the art of shopping for credit. There still is no such thing as "E-Z" credit as some lenders are so fond of advertising.

The federal "truth in lending" law does not regulate rates charged for extensions of credit; that is regulated by the states for the most part. It does, however, set forth disclosure requirements for any individual or organization that extends or arranges for credit. The two most important things that must be disclosed are the finance charge and the annual percentage rate. They must both be prominently displayed on any credit contract.

The annual percentage rate is extremely valuable in that it provides a way of comparing credit costs regardless of the dollar amount of those costs or the length of time over which payments are made. Suppose for example that you borrow $200.00 and pay $12.00 interest for the use of that money. If you use the entire amount for one year before making a lump sum payment of $212.00, your annual percentage rate is 6 percent. But if you make 12 monthly installments of principal and interest, you do not have the use of a significant portion of the money for the full year, and the annual percentage rate climbs to 11 percent. The consumer's focus of attention should be on the annual percentage rate and not on the monthly payment, which may seem deceivingly low.

The finance charge is also a very significant figure. It is the total amount being charged for borrowing the money. It will normally consist of interest, service charges and any loan fees. Suppose you want to buy a used car on credit. One car is being sold for $2,000.00 with monthly payments of $100.00, while another is $2,000.00 with monthly payments of $125.00. By looking at the finance charge you may learn that the second car is actually cheaper. Because the period of financing is only 24 months the second car costs $3,000.00 with a total finance charge of $1,000.00, while the first car, with a 36-month financing period, costs $3,600.00 with a total finance charge of $1,600.00. The law provides significant penalties for failure to disclose the annual percentage rate and the total finance charge.

In light of the existence of the "truth in lending" law the most fertile area for credit fraud has become misleading verbal representations. A consumer who reads and understands a credit contract may not be eager to pay the price being asked, so the slick salesman may see his task as diverting the customer's attention from the contract and snowing him with some verbal representations. Therefore the following maxim is the first commandment of consumerism: "If a promise is not written into a contract, it is meaningless." Regardless of what the salesman tells you about rates and fees or about prepayment options and penalties, those matters will be controlled by the written contract. If a seller or credit grantor refuses to put a statement in writing while asking you to rely on it, you should consider the statement as never having been said.

Purchasers on credit should also be aware of the holder in due course doctrine. This concept, which is so vital to the law of negotiable instruments, can be a real pitfall for the consumer. If you sign a credit contract that allows the creditor to sell the contract to a third party, such as a bank or finance company, that third party may become a holder in due course with a claim against you for payment on the contract, regardless of any defects in the original transaction. Thus if the land is flooded, the TV blows up or the engine falls out of the car, you cannot refuse to pay the third-party holder of the contract. Your dispute is only with the seller. State legislation is gradually providing some relief to consumers from the rigors of the holder in due course doctrine by chipping away at the immunity that the holder of a consumer credit contract has from claims of defects in the original transaction.

Loan churning is the practice of convincing a consumer that it is in his interest to "renew" a loan by extending it after only a short period has elapsed. In almost every case, regardless of the verbal representations made, the renewal will add considerable costs to the ultimate obligation.

Debt collection procedures can also be fraudulent in the sense that they involve misrepresentations or other improprieties. Collection notices might be falsified so as to appear to be legal documents when in fact they are not. Or a fraudulent court summons might be used to obtain a default judgment. Or debtors might be coerced into taking some action through false representations about the rights of the creditor.

The world of credit transactions can be complex but it need not be fraught with fraud. Impulse is the worst enemy of a wise credit consumer. Lack of understanding combined with neglecting to ask questions is also a formidable foe. The credit consumer's best friends are education, patience and inquisitiveness. Suspected abuses in credit transactions should be reported to the Federal Trade Commission and the state agency in your state that regulates extensions of credit.

CREDIT CARD FRAUD

It is a serious mistake to conclude that credit card fraud hurts only the issuers of the credit cards. The direct financial losses from credit card fraud may finally rest with the issuer, the merchant who accepts the card or the consumer to whom the card was originally issued. Of course, eventually the cost of such losses will always be borne by the consuming public. Thus it is very much in the interest of the consumer to educate himself concerning credit card fraud and to do his part to prevent the financial losses that result from it.

Statistics indicate that approximately 20 percent of fraud related losses in the credit card area result from credit cards issued on the basis of false applications. Another 20 percent of the losses result from cards issued to, but never received by, legitimate applicants. Such cards are stolen prior to receipt by the applicant. The remainder of credit card fraud losses involve cards that were lost by, or stolen from, card holders.

It should never be assumed that credit card fraud always involves the work of individual thieves of little sophistication. Elaborate rings, often involving multistep operations, exist to exploit the profit potential in illicit credit card use. Part of a ring may specialize in illegally acquiring credit cards while another "branch" specializes in utilization and disposition of the cards.

Many credit card schemes start with the inspection of public records to gather background information about a credit card holder. This information is then used to prepare a false application to another credit card company indicating a change of address. The company's credit check reveals a legitimate card holder, and the new card is issued. Cards issued in this manner can generally be used by the crooks for up to two months before there is any real danger of detection, and even after that the illicit cards continue to have a significant black market value.

Another common fraud against the issuer of credit cards will involve a conspiracy between a merchant and the holder of a stolen card. The holder uses the card to purchase a major appliance for $800.00, but instead of actually taking the appliance the cardholder receives $400.00 in cash from the merchant, who then collects $800.00 from the issuer of the card because of his contention that he had no way of knowing the card was stolen.

Often stolen credit cards will be used to purchase numerous appliances, which are immediately fenced for a portion of their value. Or stolen cards may be used to buy plane tickets, which are sold or exchanged for cash.

While the variety of credit card schemes is virtually endless, certain precautions can go a long way in protecting the credit card user against financial loss due to fraud. The credit card user should be wary if the regular monthly billing does not arrive, or if a charge slip enclosed in the bill indicates a total larger than that on his corresponding customer's copy (which he should always retain after each credit card transaction), or if a person is seeking to discover a credit card number under suspicious circumstances. Also, the card user should always be alert for return of the wrong card after a transaction.

The merchant accepting a credit card should always be alert to discover if the card being presented has expired, or has been altered, or if the signature on the card differs significantly from that on the charge slip. Other suspicious circumstances might involve a customer presenting a card with a credit level that seems inconsistent with his age, appearance or occupation. Finally a merchant should be wary if a card holder attempts to rush a transaction or makes numerous purchases all under the limit requiring an authorization call to the issuer.

Security procedures followed by credit card issuers and acceptors, as well as the cooperation of card users, has led to a decline in credit card fraud as a percentage of total sales. However, it's a sure bet that the criminal element that has dealt in credit card fraud will continue to make persistent efforts to develop the expertise and technology necessary to beat the improving procedural safeguards. The education and cooperation of the consuming public will remain essential in the effort to deter future schemes and minimize the cost of buying on credit.

DEBT "CONSOLIDATION" AND DEBT ADJUSTMENT FRAUDS

It is not the licensed institutional lender or debt counseling service that you need to avoid when faced with financial setbacks and creditor problems. Rather it is the operation that is new in town, that is not listed in the phone book, and that no one knows anything about that should be considered extremely suspect.

In almost every case of debt consolidation or debt adjustment fraud the victim will never actually receive a loan. Rather the firm will provide a "service" to the debtor by collecting regular payments from him and disbursing them to creditors, frequently on a pro rata basis.

The problem arises in several respects. In most cases the debt adjuster will charge a significant fee for doing very little. After all, someone deeply in debt doesn't need to pay service fees that don't help appease his creditors. Further, the creditors may not have been consulted by the debt adjuster and have not consented to less than full and timely payment of the debts. Thus the use of the debt adjustment service will not abate the relentless pressure of the bill collectors. Finally, an all-too-frequent scam involves the debt adjuster failing to make any payments to creditors but rather misappropriating the funds to his own use.

Those in debt without the funds to immediately satisfy all creditors can seek to make accommodations directly with the creditors. If unsuccessful they can consult established local debt counseling services, some of which are free. A lawyer may be successful in negotiating with the creditors and can advise the debtor of his rights and responsibilities.

DIRECTORY ADVERTISING FRAUDS

Businesses frequently find it profitable to advertise in specialized directories aimed at a particular audience of potential customers. An auto repair facility, for example, might find it advantageous to advertise in a directory distributed to insurance adjusters. Medical supply businesses want to advertise in directories distributed to doctors. There are virtually thousands of possibilities. This fact has given rise to a proliferation of business directory schemes perpetrated by groups of highly transient swindlers.

The scheme, of course, involves selling space in a business directory that will either never be printed or will be printed in such limited quantity as to be of no benefit to the business that advertises in it. Because no directory will actually be produced the only overhead is the cost of keeping one step ahead of the law. The rest is all profit.

The crooks move into town quickly, solicit ads door-to-door or from boiler room phone banks and move out of town within a matter of days. Sometimes they will implicitly or expressly misrepresent that they are affiliated with an established business directory that the business has dealt with on a regular basis. One racket even falsely claimed to be selling advertising in the yellow pages. Statistics indicate that a fraudulent business directory scheme will prosper if as few as one in twenty businesses that are approached fall for the solicitation.

Directory rackets, like many other fraudulent schemes aimed at businesses, succeed largely because of carelessness by the victim. The victim doesn't take the time to investigate the authenticity of the solicitation. He doesn't check to see if the directory has a permanent business address or check whether the organization is known in the community where it is based. He doesn't insist on examining copies of previous directories and contacting advertisers therein. He doesn't ask for a list of subscribers to the directory to verify its authenticity. Finally, he isn't appropriately suspicious when the advertising salesman he has dealt with at the same time every year for a long time is replaced by someone who contacts him at a different time of the year.

As long as businessmen remain careless, directory advertising frauds will remain profitable.

EMPLOYMENT AGENCIES

There is a good reason why many states require licensing of employment agencies. Many abuses have been perpetrated by swindlers who took on the trappings of an employment agency or career counseling service but who did not have the intent to actually assist anyone in the procurement of employment or choice of a career. Their intent was only to collect fees in return for as little as possible. If you are in a state that requires licensing of employment agencies the first precaution is to ensure that the business you're dealing with is in fact licensed. This may prevent you from being taken by a truly fly-by-night operation.

The contract the job seeker signs with an employment agency is extremely important. It reveals the fees involved for finding employment and the obligations and responsibilities of the respective parties. If the business makes verbal representations that are inconsistent with or in addition to the written contract, something is wrong. To be enforceable all terms and conditions should be in the contract. Make sure you read and understand the contract so you won't be paying half of the first five years' wages to the employment agency or be paying the agency long after you quit the job because it was not suitable.

Make sure to determine whether the organization you are dealing with is actually in the business of securing employment or merely in the business of job counseling or résumé preparation. In the late 1960's and early 1970's career counseling services were abundant and many collected substantial fees for psychological testing to determine career aptitudes and for counseling services with supposed guidance counselors. They claimed to have contacts with the upper echelons of American industry. In fact their contacts were very limited and their résumé files collected nothing but dust.

One employment agency racket involved collecting $250.00 fees to secure high-paying, exotic and glamorous employment overseas. In fact the jobs secured were either fictitious or anything but glamorous. Such firms can only survive a relatively short period before moving on, so dealing with an established and reputable agency will help you stay clear of such pitfalls.

FALSE BILLING SCHEMES

It is the goal of any false billing scheme to induce an individual or business to pay a bill that is fraudulent in some respect. Thus the essence of any such scheme is the perpetrator's reliance on the inefficiency of the person or business he seeks to victimize. He relies on sloppy bookkeeping, inattentive employees and perhaps most of all the failure of one arm of a bureaucracy to know what another arm is doing.

In its rarest form a false billing scheme will involve a mass mailing to businesses for goods or services never received. For example, a business might receive a bill for advertising in a publication connected with their line of business. The bookkeeper may not suspect anything because it would certainly not be unusual for the business to advertise in such a publication. So he never consults the person in charge of advertising before sending a check to the post office box set up by the perpetrators of the scheme.

Another scenario that is very prevalent would find a business receiving a phone call (usually long distance) from someone who expressly or implicitly indicates that he is affiliated with a local office supply business and warns of an impending drastic increase in the price of a product needing periodic replenishing, such as toner dispersant for copying machines. He convinces the business that it will be a savings to order a large supply of the product prior to the price increase. The product (generally of inferior quality) is delivered with an invoice indicating payment is to be made to a local post office box or to an out-of-town address. This is the critical point. If the address does not raise undue suspicion, the bill will be paid. It is not until the local office supply store calls a month later to say that it's time to reorder the product that the scheme is discovered. When detected at an earlier stage the quickest way to deter such schemes is to keep the supplies sent without paying for them.

An ambitious false billing scheme might entail a phone call to a large manufacturing facility. The caller purports to be a representative from a government agency who is conducting an energy conservation survey. He asks to talk to the head of the maintenance department, who is delighted by the attention paid to him by a government bureaucrat. The caller asks how many light bulbs the facility uses, when they are ordered, who they are purchased from and what was the most recent price paid for them. He thanks the head of maintenance for his cooperation in the survey. A bill is then prepared for an appropriate amount purporting to be from the usual supplier but with a different address. It is sent at an appropriate point in time, preferably shortly before the authentic bill arrives. The schemers hope against hope that the company's bureaucracy will fail and the bill will be paid.

As might be expected, large companies with systematic and often computerized protection against false billing schemes are not the usual victims. Nor is the very small business where the sole proprietor has his hand on the checkbook at all times and deals personally with all his suppliers. Rather it is generally a medium-sized firm suffering from growing pains that is most susceptible to the scam.

An effective system of record keeping by an accounts payable department goes a long way toward the prevention of financial loss due to false billing. Any such system should include a cross-reference of the actual address for the supplier against the address on the invoice received.

INSURANCE FRAUD

Consider the various types of insurance available. Just a few include health, life, auto, home, unemployment, Medicare and liability. Now imagine the types of fraud that can be perpetrated in *each* area. You begin to get the picture.

Unethical salesmen can pressure people into buying unneeded and unaffordable policies. Thieves can collect for policies never issued. False claims can be made for property damage and for fraudulent injuries. Medicare, Medicaid and welfare plans can be victimized through false or fraudulent claims, as can Social Security. False claims can be manufactured for unemployment benefits. And moving up the ladder, even the insurance companies themselves can be used as vehicles of fraud. Consider the Equity Funding scandal of 1973. The company created an illusion of growth by loading its computers with imaginary insurance premiums from nonexistent customers. This growth attracted new investors, who poured money into the firm and created some legitimate growth, thereby fueling the fraud. Upon the firm's collapse many people lost a great deal of money.

An extensive discussion of insurance fraud would require a book in itself. This treatment of the subject is designed merely to point out the general nature of several insurance fraud schemes and to highlight some suspicious circumstances indicative of such schemes.

Insurance, by its very nature, lends itself to abuse. There is an impersonality attached to large insurance companies, which tends to vitiate normal guilt feelings. It's all right to steal from the insurance company. *It* has lots of money and besides, haven't you already paid the company? This one inflated claim won't really hurt anyone. So the insurance industry is subject to fraud by the dishonest claimant and by the professional thief.

Just a few examples will illustrate the point. The first involves the more bloodthirsty individual in our society. This charmer has his wife killed to collect the insurance premiums. Maybe he fakes a home burglary or a robbery to cover his tracks. Tidy sums are involved.

Or take someone with a less vicious bent. He merely slaps the side of a motor vehicle hard enough to make a loud noise and then falls to the ground, mortally injured. The injury may be faked through accessories or he may attempt to convince a legitimate doctor of the serious back or whiplash injury. He knows all the symptoms. Fraudulent claims can be made to cover hospital and medical expenses as well as damages for lost work and pain and suffering. But that requires a certain sophistication and acting ability on the part of the perpetrator.

Others may choose merely to utilize claims for property damage. Take the taxi company that turns in several claims on the same cab for the same damage merely by changing license plates on the vehicle.

You prefer a more sophisticated scheme? Take the woman who, along with other members of her family, derives a very healthy income by making false welfare claims under thirty-seven separate identities.

Not sophisticated enough? Let's discuss specialization. For this scheme we need the services of unscrupulous professionals. Our cast of characters includes doctors, lawyers, nurses, hospital administrators and claims adjustors. A willing participant has a minor automobile accident. The claims adjustor inflates the damages to the point where the vehicle is a total loss. He then contacts A-1 Wrecking, which takes the car, makes minor repairs and resells it. Collection is made on the insurance policy and in addition a profit is made on the resale.

The victim has already been taken from the scene by All-Right Ambulance. The victim is transported, sitting up, to Community Profit Hospital. The insurance company is charged for lifesaving equipment, including the use of oxygen and other expensive disposable items. The victim is walked through at the hospital and assigned a bed. He stays for two weeks and leaves wearing a neck brace. Hospital expenses include emergency room care and numerous extras. During his hospital stay no one visited the victim but a doctor submits bills for services rendered totaling several thousand dollars.

After the victim's release he visits the doctor once and receives no treatment. Billing is made for several visits and for expensive treatments. A pharmacy bills for prescriptions never dispensed to the victim. And now it's time for the victim to visit his attorney, who files suit for all these damages along with additional thousands for loss of work, loss of consortium, loss of earning power and pain and suffering. Of course, all this is well documented and the insurance company pays. It pays thousands of dollars for this *one* victim.

A variation works well in bilking the government out of Medicare benefits through fraudulent billings for treatments never performed. And the two can even be used in concert with the medical costs being assessed against the appropriate government plan and then a suit being brought against a third party who may have been the driver of the other car. Sometimes that driver receives a piece of the action for his cooperation. That should be sufficient for a sophisticated operation.

Take a couple more quick examples. One might be the disappearing insured. Here the insured is mysteriously killed. His beneficiary collects the cash and the two turn up months later in Rio de Janeiro.

Or how about a sheme involving liability insurance. Here we have the famous "slip and fall" in a grocery store. Our victim slips on a small piece of ice and is seriously injured. The store's insurance pays.

There is also the policyholder as the victim. Those who are above age 65 are especially vulnerable to this scam — which, by the way, is probably not illegal in many states even though it is highly unethical.

A salesman contacts a 72-year-old widow who lives alone. He plays upon her natural desires not to burden anyone in the case of severe illness and sells her a supplemental policy to cover any costs not paid by Medicare or Medicaid.

It was an easy sale. So he goes back again and sells other supplemental policies. Or he passes her name on to another salesman. Over the course of several months she is sold forty-five policies, including seven that have maternity benefits.

Shortly her ability to pay debts is severely restricted as she is paying various insurance companies hundreds of dollars per month in unnecessary insurance premiums. It is at this point that the family may discover what has occurred and move to remedy the problem. Seldom does the victim realize he has been bamboozled or if he does realize it, there seldom is a report made to the authorities.

A most insidious form of Medicare or Social Security fraud is perpetrated by swindlers posing as government employees who convince elderly persons that they need to cough up a certain amount of money to insure their continued eligibility for benefits. They are confused by the hard sell and typically don't check with local Medicare or Social Security offices in time to decipher the scam.

Insurance also plays a large role in the construction industry. Everyone associated with a major project wants his interest protected. So policies are written to cover all contingencies. That includes the theft of $25,000.00 worth of materials from a job site. The insurance is paid and the contractor "buys" new material. It's a quick way to pocket $25,000.00.

Last there is insurance fraud in connection with one of the fastest growing crimes in the country — arson. A partially finished building, on which the contractor underbid, burns to the ground. Insurance proceeds pull the contractor out. A failing business burns. A business that has been milked dry by organized crime burns. A man's house burns. And in each instance the property is heavily insured.

There are no reliable statistics available on the dollar losses directly traced to insurance fraud. Probably no one knows the full extent of the problem. But in the end you pay in increased insurance premiums and higher costs for combating the insurance fraud problem.

And you may also pay when you submit a legitimate claim that could be fraudulent; because of the prevalence of fraud the insurance company spends unnecessary dollars fighting the claim. The ultimate problem is that in each case above, the claim could have been legitimate.

There are numerous warning signs of false insurance claims. Among the most suspicious is the frequent and consistent utilization by claimants of the same lawyer-physician combination. Other significant red flags include the intervention of an attorney at an extremely early stage of the matter, a claimant who seems extremely well versed about the claim adjustment process, a claimant in a personal injury case who seems all too willing to settle for the "nuisance value" of the case, a doctor who refuses to itemize his bill for treatment in an insurance claim case or a patient who is treated at a hospital operated by his physician.

Insurance purchasers as well as insurance companies may be the victims of frauds perpetrated by dishonest agents. One such scheme involves agents selling high-risk automobile insurance policies and failing to inform the company. They will collect premiums directly from the insureds without submitting them to the company. Such schemes are almost always detected when a driver gets in an accident and the agent is forced to backdate a policy. An insured should be suspicious if he never receives anything from the insurance company, including a policy, and always makes payments directly to the agent. The backdating of policies will almost always involve forging certain documents by the agent. One problem for law enforcement combating such schemes has been the reluctance of insurance companies to report crime by their agents because they believe it reflects negatively on the company.

However, the insurance industry as a whole is expending considerable time, effort and money to combat fraud. Law enforcement is also becoming more sophisticated in its approach to insurance related crimes. But the role of the insurance customer in spotting possible fraud and bringing it to the attention of law enforcement cannot be overestimated. This brand of white collar crime is very costly to society as a whole, and everyone benefits by its detection and prosecution.

OFFSHORE BANKS

The term "offshore" has become popular in financial circles as a term to connote a place where business can avoid the burdens of taxation and regulation that seem so pervasive in the industrial world. But for thousands of disillusioned investors and frustrated police agencies the term offshore is synonymous with fraud.

The Channel islands, such as Sark, Guernsey and Alderney, as well as Bermuda, the Bahamas and several other islands, are all part of the British Empire. However, they enjoy considerable autonomy in the establishment of commercial law. This autonomy makes such islands attractive for international business ventures whose principal selling point is that investments can be hidden from the prying eyes of taxing authorities.

Offshore havens received an undeserved appearance of legitimacy in the 1960's when several large international corporations utilized them to shelter profits. Ford, ITT, Exxon and others set up "captive" insurance companies. The corporations sent untaxed profits from American operations to the dummy insurance companies on the pretense of establishing reserves to cover future casualty losses. The money was in turn invested in overseas operations to procure additional tax-free profits.

This technique led many financial managers to recognize the potential of offshore operations. Mutual funds headquartered offshore sold shares all over the world, although they could not legally sell in the United States because of the failure to meet Securities and Exchange Commission requirements. However, the lack of scrutiny from government overseers that seemed so attractive to investors also had a major drawback. No one was in a position to realize that investors' funds were being diverted into other ventures run by the same men who had founded the mutual funds. By 1970, the offshore mutual funds had collapsed, leaving thousands of investors with large financial losses in their wake.

It then occurred to enterprising con men that slowly siphoning investors' money was an inefficient way to fun and profits. An offshore operation that was so totally corrupt that it stole every penny of investors' money was far more efficient, involved less paperwork and was equally unlikely to result in legal sanctions that were worthy of concern. Thus was born such noble financial institutions as the infamous Bank of Sark.

Since the Bank of Sark wasn't really a bank it didn't need to have real assets or pay real interest on deposits. But it had to make people believe that it had money and paid tax sheltered interest. This was readily accomplished by producing falsified balance sheets showing impressive sums. Of course, the secrecy the bank boasted of required that such records never be subjected to the scrutiny of outside auditors.

A mutual fund was set up that gave custody of all its assets to the Bank of Sark and the shares of the fund were peddled very aggressively in Europe. Meanwhile, millions of dollars in drafts on the Bank of Sark were accepted by other banks and major corporations. None of them were paid by the Bank of Sark. Even after the Bailiwick of Guernsey removed the Bank of Sark from its company registry for calling itself a bank when it in fact wasn't one, its bad paper continued to circulate as a reminder that, in the financial world, as elsewhere, things aren't always as they appear to be.

There are many other sad tales to be told in the history of offshore banks. They will remain legendary in the annals of white collar crime as a monument to the daring of professional swindlers who rob the public with fast talk and fountain pens rather than guns. Suffice it to say that the very feature that is supposed to make such investments attractive, lack of oversight by government regulators, is also the feature that makes them a very risky proposition.

While law enforcement has won sporadic victories in the battle against these large-scale frauds, final victory requires that the investigators and prosecutors who fight the battles develop as much expertise in their fields as the swindlers have in theirs. It also requires that the legitimate financial community develop the sophistication necessary to discriminate against the swindlers and prevent them from blending in so well with the landscape of respectable business.

TAX SHELTER FRAUDS

The proceeds of economic crime generally go unreported and untaxed, so it is not surprising that those crooks who have long been familiar with the techniques of tax evasion would eventually recognize the potential for selling fraudulent tax shelters as a way to reap greater untaxed profits.

Perpetrators of tax shelter fraud who have thus far been apprehended seem to have specialized in one of two techniques. The first preys upon unsophisticated taxpayers of moderate means while the other preys upon those of substantial means who have at least convinced themselves that they have some sophistication in tax matters.

A typical example of how a crook preys upon the unsophisticated taxpayer will suffice to show his basic approach. He fashions himself as a "financial consultant." When you meet him at a public or private gathering he is dressed to kill and his personality is attractive. He subtly maneuvers the conversation to financial matters and tells you he specializes in tax planning for individuals. He uses plenty of big words in hopes of convincing you of his vast knowledge of the tax laws. In fact, his knowledge is derived from a three-hour course for income tax return preparers. But he is well schooled in the art of salesmanship and before you know it you have an appointment with him tomorrow night at your home (he doesn't have an office) to discuss your particular situation.

He arrives with a briefcase full of materials and after an hour of financial revelations on your part he boldly announces that he can show you how to save $4,000 in taxes this year and additional thousands in years to come by setting up trusts for yourself and your children. The cost to you is $2,000 and that in itself is deductible according to him. He assures you that the Internal Revenue Service has recognized this means of tax avoidance. Like most people you've heard there are tax advantages to be derived from the use of trusts, but that is the extent of your sophistication. You don't know the difference between revocable and irrevocable trusts and the tax implications of each. The price sounds like a bargain so you write him a check.

Several weeks later you receive his tax shelter "kit" in the mail. You're slightly mystified by the written disclaimers that weren't previously verbalized but you're also pleasantly surprised at the simple instructions you are asked to follow. You set up a bank account for yourself and each of your children, call them trusts and appoint yourself trustee. Money channeled through the "trusts" will be tax-free. It's all so simple. In fact, it is much too simple. The necessary requirements for an irrevocable trust with tax advantages are simply not present and in a contest with the IRS you will lose, quickly and certainly. You've been sold a bogus bill of goods. By the way, when you attempt to contact your financial consultant regarding your adversity with the IRS you find that he's moved on to share his knowledge with others and he's left no forwarding address. Your friends who also paid for his tax "advice" can't seem to locate him either.

Where did you go wrong? Start with your failure to check his credentials. Certified public accountants, tax lawyers and other qualified professionals may not come cheap but at least they know what the big words mean. There is no substitute for true professional competence. Look to them for anything more than simple tax return preparation assistance. Further, when you pay for tax planning you should expect more than a "do it yourself" kit. You should expect preparation of documents and a full explanation of potential problems with the IRS, including a discussion of previous IRS rulings and tax court opinions.

As previously mentioned, the person who believes he has some knowledge of tax matters and who is actively on the lookout for tax shelters may also be the target of a fraudulent scheme. You're approached to make an investment in a program that, because of its nature, has both large potential returns and significant tax advantages. A favorite is investments in energy production situations such as oil exploration and solar fuels, because these types of investment do have legitimate tax savings possibilities. For your $15,000 investment you are told you can expect to receive tax credits or deductions of up to $40,000 the first year.

The problem, of course, is that this investment is not legitimate. There is no oil exploration or solar fuels production taking place. If "tax-free" returns are forthcoming chances are it's a Ponzi scheme in which the return to the investor is merely money provided by subsequent investors. (*See* the section on Ponzi Schemes.) Once the scam is uncovered your tax deduction moves to another place on the IRS form and becomes much less glamorous — a loss due to theft.

Most persons who have thus far been burned by this form of tax shelter scheme can attribute their loss to their failure to use the protection available to investors through various regulatory agencies. Insist on evidence that the investment has passed muster with the appropriate securities commission and other regulatory agencies and that the offeror provide a genuine opinion of counsel concerning the potential tax benefits. Until evidence of this nature is forthcoming, don't invest. And don't invest without seeking the advice of a professional tax adviser. Deal with licensed brokers and licensed salesmen. Don't deal with the wheeler-dealer friend of your cousin who brags that he hasn't paid taxes in ten years and whose only license is a license to steal.

7

Miscellaneous "Classic Cons"

CONFIDENCE GAMES

This book describes a wide variety of fraudulent schemes; the tendency of the uninitiated might be to refer to all the schemes as confidence games and all the schemers as confidence men. But those terms have a precise connotation and should not be utilized too loosely by someone who considers himself to be knowledgeable in the sociology of fraud.

Technically speaking, a confidence game is a scheme that has certain essential characteristics. In almost every con game the victim (called the mark) is allowed to profit by dishonest means and then is induced to make a large investment that is appropriated by the con men. In fact the real genius behind con games is that the victim must virtually admit criminal intentions himself if he wishes to prosecute the swindlers. This principle is usually behind the simplest con as well as the most sophisticated. Hence the truism, "You can't con an honest man."

BIG CONS. The family of confidence games consists of big cons, of which there are essentially three, and a plethora of short cons. In the first half of the twentieth century the three big cons, the wire, the payoff and the rag, have exacted an incredible financial toll from a gullible and greedy public. The less ambitious short cons have provided and continue to provide a means of maintaining a comfortable life-style for many grifters.

Big cons are distinguishable from short cons in that the mark is "put on the send," which means he is persuaded to go to a bank or somewhere else to get funds, whereas in a short con the "touch" is generally limited to the amount the mark has with him. As a result, big cons generally involve larger overhead and larger profits. They also typically involve the operation of a "big store" manned by a "con insideman miscommunicates information to the bettor. The bettor loses all his money when he is mistakenly told by the telegraph mob." A big store is a business establishment, usually a poolroom that takes race bets or a broker's office, that is contrived only for the operation of the con game. The con mob consists of the personnel operating the big store, including insidemen and a staff of "ropers" and shills. While big cons are not dead, they are well past their prime — not so much because the public is smarter or because law enforcement is more effective but because of the passing of a generation of con artists who earned a reputation as the masters of chicanery. But even today the con man remains the artistocrat of the criminal element of society. He is still suave and intelligent, and he is still hard to catch.

Any well-planned big con will progress through certain steps that are readily identifiable. Step one is locating a well-heeled victim (finding the mark). Step two is gaining the victim's confidence (playing the con). Third is steering the victim to an insideman (roping the mark). Fourth is the insideman showing the victim how to make a large amount of money dishonestly (telling the tale). Step five is allowing the mark to profit by the dishonesty (the convincer). Step six is determining how much the victim will invest (the breakdown). Step seven is sending him to the bank or elsewhere to get the money (the send). The next step is taking the victim into the big store and fleecing him (the touch). Next is sending him on his way (blowing him off). An optional step, not necessarily last in time, is ensuring the law will not interfere (the fix).

The oldest of the big cons, and perhaps the most well known, is the wire. It is certainly the one most popularized in literature and the movies. The idea for the wire developed in the late 1800's when certain telegraph operators began making money by convincing gullible race fans to advance funds to help them tap telegraph wires, obtain advance information on race results and hold up the transmission of the results until the fan placed a bet on the winner. No doubt some were actually capable of the feat and shared the winnings with the bettors. But actually performing the scam was complex and dangerous in terms of possible legal consequences. It became much more effective and profitable to take the bettor's money on the pretense of pulling off the telegraph tap scam and then abscond, relying on the fact that the bettor would not call the police and report his own involvement in illegal activities. However, it was not until professional grifters applied this idea to the concept of the big store that the scam was refined so as to become an art form among confidence men.

Once the mark is convinced the race results are being delayed and is willing to invest his own money he can readily be played against a fake bookmaker operating out of a fake poolroom manned by participants in the con game. Ropers roam the countryside looking for marks to play against the store. The wire culminates when an interceptor to put his money on Seabiscuit to win instead of Seabiscuit to place. Thus the blame for the loss is placed on a single incompetent middleman and the mark may not suspect a rip-off. Soon thereafter the mark is "blown off" by being informed that the cops or Western Union detectives have discovered the gimmick. Afraid of being arrested for his involvement, the mark is willing to leave town quickly, leaving his money behind to be divided up by the con mob.

The payoff is actually a variation of the same theme utilized in the wire. Rather than the alleged interception of transmitted race results it involves convincing the mark that the insider is part of a network that fixes races and that money can be made by betting on the fixed races. But the same big store is used — a poolroom with bookmaking in the back room. The mark is fleeced when an insider mistakenly communicates that a horse will win instead of place. The blow off may even involve one insider allegedly shooting the party responsible for the mistake, leading the mark to believe that other insiders are as upset as he and further leading him to flee the jurisdiction lest a police investigation of the shooting could involve him. This method of blowing off the mark is called cacklebladder, a name derived from a small bladder filled with chicken blood that the insideman conceals in his mouth until he is "shot."

The rag is an adaptation of the payoff. The principal elements of the payoff are applied to a deal in stocks or other securities. It may not be until the roper has gained the confidence of the mark and consulted with other members of the con mob that it is decided which game to play him for. He will likely be played for the game he knows the least about, i.e., a stockbroker will be played for the payoff. The roper might meet the mark on a train, a plane or a subway. He identifies him as someone with money who is gullible and then initiates an acquaintanceship. The roper will eventually introduce the mark to another insider, who appears to be a wheeler-dealer in the stock market. The roper and the mark learn from the insider about a surefire way to make money in the market. The insider reveals that he has access to reliable inside information and has a direct line to some stock manipulators in New York. He invites the roper and the mark to invest a small amount with him and he brings them back twice as much money the next day. After doing this two or three times the insider introduces the mark to the big store for the rag. It is a precise replica of a broker's office. The con mob staffs it as brokers and customers. Eventually the mark is persuaded to produce a large amount of money to invest. The roper relays a message from the insider to the mark telling him to buy a certain stock on margin. Only after the purchase is made does the mark learn that the message was fouled up by the roper or the insider. He was supposed to sell short!

The blow off is essentially the same. The mark is told that law enforcement authorities are onto the stock manipulation scheme and bearing in on those involved. Some insidemen may even be arrested by con mob members posing as police detectives.

Big cons are well-written plays based on well-written scripts. Each of the actors knows his role and his lines — except for the mark. He doesn't know his part and doesn't know the plot involves a financial travesty for him. It is the complexity and the elaborateness of the big con that has made it the most glamorous of fraud schemes and that has made the confidence man the most glamorous of swindlers. The reaction of most readers will be to conclude that they could never be so naive as to fall for the big con. But wherever there is a person with money with the desire for more money there is the potential for a big-time swindle.

SHORT CONS. As mentioned previously a short con game is generally one in which the mark is taken only for the amount he has on his person. The mark is not "put on the send." However, creative confidence men sometimes utilize the send in what is otherwise essentially a short con. Thus it is perhaps most accurate to say that the short con is any confidence game except the wire, the payoff and the rag. There are literally hundreds of short cons and it would be impossible to cover each of them in a book of less than biblical proportions. Therefore, only a few of the many short cons will be discussed.

One frequently utilized short con is the smack. It is a low-overhead operation. The roper meets the mark at a train station or airport while the mark is killing time waiting for a train or plane. The mark and the roper run across an insideman who is posing as a very gullible traveler. Pursuant to a challenge by the insider the three get to tossing coins for money with the odd man being the winner. The roper then slips the mark a weighted coin that always comes up heads and uses one himself that always comes up tails, thereby ensuring one of them will always win. The insider pretends never to catch on and in frustration eventually challenges the other two to put up all the money on one toss. The roper handles all the money, including that put up by the mark, and tells the mark they should meet secretly at a particular place to divide the winnings. Of course the only money to be divided will be the mark's money and that will be divided by the roper and insideman. They will then wait until the mark has caught his train or plane before searching out a new mark.

Another common short con is the tat. The tat involves a crooked die with fives on four sides and sixes on two sides. The con men frequent bars and nightclubs and sucker unsuspecting parties into a game where each person puts up a sum of money and rolls dice, with the pot going to the person with the highest total for each roll of the dice. Sleight of hand is utilized to substitute the crooked die at appropriate times.

The tip is also a short con for gamblers and involves some dexterity with cards. The roper gains the confidence of a mark and proposes to assist him in setting up a third person in a poker game.

The roper loses early and gets out. He then gives the mark signals to inform him of cards held by the third person, who is an insideman. The insideman exhibits lots of money and the scheme climaxes with a showdown hand involving large raises. The roper miscommunicates a signal to the mark, who loses all his money. A very gullible mark may believe the roper's story about the mix-up and come back for more after visiting his bank.

The autograph is a short con in which the mark is induced to sign a piece of paper that, unknown to him, is a negotiable instrument.

A variety of short cons is the bread and butter of fly-by-night carnival operators. One such con is three-card monte. The task of the customer is to pick a queen from three cards dealt face down. The mark observes some insidemen playing and winning. He is approached by one of the players who says he will crimp the corner of the queen so that the mark can always identify it. When the stakes get appropriately high the insideman who is running the game cleverly removes the crimped queen and crimps one of the other two cards. When he loses, the mark will be unlikely to complain because he lost while trying to cheat.

The list of short cons goes on and on. They're called by short and descriptive terms like the hot seat, the money box, the last turn, the huge duke, the wipe, the spud, the bat, the rocks, the tale, the lemon, the ducats and the high pitch. Just about every conceivable method for fleecing a mark has been perfected in the form of a short con. The mark may or may not recognize the fact he's been swindled.

One final scheme that deserves mention, but that is not technically a big con or a short con, is the hype (also known as laying the note). It is a skilled short-change racket and as such lacks a basic element of a con game. The mark is not acting dishonestly at the time he is fleeced. The crook, who is frequently a con man taking a brief respite from con games, utilizes sleight of hand, misdirection and confusion in numerous ways to consistently walk away from the cash register with a profit. Victims generally never understand precisely how the short change took place. Experts say the best way for a cashier to combat the hype is to slowly and completely execute each proposed transaction. Don't let the "customer" change his mind in midstream. Have the customer's money from one transaction in the cash register before undertaking the next transaction he proposes.

MISSING HEIR SCHEME

At one time or another everyone has dreamed about going to the mailbox one day and finding a letter informing him that a long-lost uncle has died and left him a large sum of money. Such dreams are of considerable assistance to unscrupulous swindlers in the perpetration of what is generally known as a missing heir scheme.

Suppose that Ralph Brown of Anywhere, California, receives an official-looking letter from a company called Probate Investigators, Ltd. The letter informs Ralph that a Mr. Reginald Brown of New York City has died intestate (without a will) and that it is believed that Ralph may be one of his long-lost relatives and an heir to a portion of his large estate. The company offers to investigate the matter for the purpose of protecting Ralph's interests and eventually asks for either a small fee or a sum to "cover expenses." Ralph's never heard of anyone in his family named Reginald, but he does believe his family's American roots go back to New York. Besides he's a gambler at heart. So he pays the small fee of $25.00 as a long-shot gamble. Who knows, it may pay off. Nothing ventured nothing gained is his attitude. Several months go by and Ralph doesn't hear from the investigative firm. Then one day at work he overhears a co-worker Josephine Brown talking about the fact that she had paid $25.00 to find out if she was an heir to the estate of an alleged relative named Reginald Brown. Ralph grabs the phone book and makes a few calls. His suspicions are confirmed. Everyone named Brown in the city of Anywhere received the same letter he did. So goes the typical missing heir scheme.

The first thing that someone who receives a "dream come true" letter such as that described should do is be skeptical. The second thing is to do a little investigating of your own. Find out if the person named did in fact die and if an estate is being probated. If so, contact the party presently administering the estate to see if there are in fact missing heirs being sought. If so, see if the administrator has assigned any firm the task of investigating or is doing it himself. Once you've contacted an administrator for the estate you can acquire information that will help you determine if there is any possibility that you might in fact be a missing heir with a legitimate claim to an inheritance.

OBITUARY FRAUDS

It is no secret that investment counselors, real estate agents and other business people frequently keep an eye on the obituary column of the local paper. Death frequently means changes in the lives of survivors and those changes might entail the need for certain business services. Con artists have also traditionally relied on the obituary columns to find vulnerable victims for some of their slickest and most despicable schemes.

Perhaps the oldest and most famous obituary scam entails a Bible salesman showing up at the door of a recently widowed woman. He asks for her husband Harry knowing full well that Harry has recently died. When informed of Harry's demise by the widow he explains that before Harry died he ordered a bible as a present for her. He shows the widow the Bible with her name engraved on it and says Harry hadn't paid the $50.00 for it yet. Overcome with emotion, and somehow managing to forget the fact that Harry was one of the world's most outspoken agnostics, the widow gives the salesman the $50.00 so that she can have it to remember her dear departed. The same Bible could be purchased in town for $10.00.

While the Bible scheme is not as prevalent today as it once was, the basic theory is timeless. There presently exist numerous schemes that involve billing widows or widowers for products their spouses supposedly purchased shortly before their death. Always investigate bills of questionable origin closely before allowing the deceased's estate to pay them or before paying them yourself.

Any scheme that preys upon the survivors of a recently deceased person, whether or not the victim's name was actually found in an obituary column, can properly be called an obituary fraud or "widow scheme." It is fact rather than sexist to point out that widows have more frequently been victims than have widowers. Survivors who have inherited considerable sums may be besieged by a variety of schemes attempting to sell any number of worthless services. There is no substitute for the advice of trusted and experienced persons in times of trauma. They can assist in the task of distinguishing between those with a legitimate service to offer and those who are out to pull off an obituary scam.

PIGEON DROP

Above all else a successful pigeon drop scheme requires a pigeon — a highly gullible and unperceiving victim. Police statistics, which are not always wholly reliable, indicate that the scheme is most frequently perpetrated against the elderly. While some versions of the scheme rely upon the victim's greed and dishonesty, others rely upon his desire to help deter crime.

One typical and very unsophisticated method involves a "chance" contact on the street between the crook and his potential victim, the pigeon. The crook approaches the victim and explains that he is new in town and has found a large sum of money. He shows the victim an envelope that does in fact contain a large sum of money. He will offer some reason why it is necessary to have the victim's assistance in finding the owner and offers half of the proceeds to the victim if the owner is not found. He states his desire to put the new-found money into the victim's possession while an owner is sought and the police are contacted, but states further that he feels the victim should give the finder of the money some cash to hold during the interim in order to manifest his honesty in the matter. The victim sees this as reasonable and extracts money from his bank account. He gives the finder the "collateral" when he is handed the envelope. The "finder" quickly disappears as the victim discovers the envelope no longer contains real cash.

More sophisticated versions of the "found money" pigeon drop scheme might involve another insider who plots with the victim to take the money from the apparently gullible finder through a rigged card game or some other device. But in the end the victim will still be called upon to show his good faith by placing a large amount of money in the hands of the finder or other insider. Or perhaps the victim's money will be given to the finder or insider for safekeeping from another crook who has become involved. In any event it will be taken and divided among the crooks. The victim, if he is inclined to go to the police, will not know enough about the crooks to assist much in their apprehension. As ludicrous as these schemes sound, and as much as they depend on incredibly gullible victims, they have been successfully perpetrated thousands of times.

Another classic pigeon drop scheme involves asking the victim to assist in the apprehension of a dishonest bank employee. The victim may receive a phone call from someone claiming to be an officer of the victim's bank, or perhaps a bank examiner. The victim is asked as a law-abiding citizen of the community to cooperate with the police by withdrawing a sizable sum from his account and delivering it to a police undercover officer at a particular time and location. The secrecy of the investigation requires that the victim keep quiet about the matter for several days. This provides more than enough time for the crooks to be out of town before the pigeon becomes suspicious. Many are the victims who were caught by thieves while trying to assist in the apprehension of an imaginary thief.

The potential victim of a pigeon drop can avoid his contemplated fate by perceiving the very obvious warning signs: the chance to make quick money and/or the request to obtain a sum of money from a bank and hand it over to a virtual stranger. Fortunately, successful pigeon drops seem to be on the decrease.

The Language of Fraud and Deceit

bait and switch — A merchandising scheme whereby a merchant lures a customer into his store with an attractive but insincere offer to sell a product or service and then switches the customer to an unadvertised product that involves a higher profit to himself.

big con — A confidence game in which the victim is allowed to leave the presence of the perpetrators in order to procure funds, as contrasted to a short con where the victim is taken only for an amount the victim has on his person when contacted. The three recognized big cons are the wire, the payoff and the rag.

big store — A fake business establishment used in the perpetration of a big con, usually a poolroom or stockbroker's office.

boiler room — An office location where several telephones are temporarily installed for the purpose of contacting persons and persuading them to give their money to perpetrators of a fraudulent scheme.

bunko (or bunco) — A general term to connote fraudulent schemes where a victim is fleeced at a rigged game or otherwise.

bust-out — A fraudulent scheme whereby a business is formed and acquires assets, generally on credit or through investors, and then abruptly absconds with the perpetrators of the scheme profiting by converting the assets of the business to themselves. The scheme resembles a bankruptcy fraud without a formal bankruptcy.

check kiting — A fraudulent scheme involving the manipulation of bad checks between two or more banks for the purpose of stealing money from the banks.

con game (or confidence game) — Any scheme in which the victim is induced to invest his money in an attempt to profit by dishonest means and then is fleeced by the perpetrators of the scheme.

con mob — The persons who are involved in the perpetration of a con game, including ropers, insidemen and the personnel of a big store.

"cooling off" period — A three-day period of time during which a consumer has the right to cancel a sale made to him at his residence.

corporate shell — A corporation that has failed and became dormant, without substantial assets, but that has not been formally dissolved and retains the right to issue additional stock.

fence — Purchaser or conduit of stolen property.

fifty-percenter — A service station attendant who sabotages automobiles in exchange for a percentage of the profits derived from the sale of new parts caused by the sabotage.

fix — To influence law enforcement authorities by a bribe or otherwise to overlook a violation of the law.

fleece — To swindle.

grifter — A professional criminal who lives by his wits. His schemes are collectively called grift.

guilt inducement schemes — A deceptive scheme that preys upon the victim's psychological insecurity or physical inadequacy, such as obesity.

hanging bad paper — Writing bad checks and writing forged checks.

launder — The process of converting the proceeds of crime into legitimate businesses.

low-balling — A repair scheme in which a business persuades a customer to leave an item for repair on the basis of an opinion that the problem is a minor one, and then later convinces the customer that the problem is major and sells him unnecessary repairs.

mark — A victim or intended victim of a confidence game.

obituary frauds — A fraudulent scheme in which the swindler preys upon the survivors of a recently deceased person.

the payoff — A big con where the wealthy victim believes he is involved in profiting by betting on fixed races and is fleeced when he bets a large amount on a particular race on the basis of mistaken instructions.

pigeon — The victim of a fraudulent scheme, in particular the victim of a scheme known as a pigeon drop.

Ponzi scheme — A fraudulent investment scheme in which investors are paid substantial returns from the funds collected from subsequent investors, thereby inducing still others to commit funds to the nonexistent investment.

pyramid promotional scheme — A scheme utilizing a pyramid or chain process in which a participant derives a profit primarily by the recruitment of other persons who give consideration for the privilege of recruiting still others, rather than by the sale of a product or service.

the rag — A big con in which the victim believes he is profiting by investing in stocks that are being manipulated by insiders and then is fleeced when he invests a large amount of money on the basis of mistaken instructions.

roper — The member of a con mob who locates a victim and brings him into a con game, usually by introducing him to an insideman.

short con — As contrasted to a big con, a confidence game where the victim is taken only for the amount of money he has with him when contacted by the perpetrators of the scheme.

song shark — A song publisher or record company that derives profits from fees paid by the musician to have his song published or recorded and does not depend on sales to make a profit.

Tennessee land fraud — A scheme whereby worthless land grant deeds are sold to persons who are unaware that the interests transferred by the deed are inferior to the interests of persons who actually reside on the land. The scheme is most common in areas of the South where land grants were common.

touch — The taking of money from the victim of a fraudulent scheme.

vanity publisher — A book publisher that derives profits from fees paid by the author to have his book published and does not depend on sales of the book to make a profit.

white collar crime — Crime that involves the utilization of the intellect without use of force or violence or threat thereof.

the wire — A big con in which the victim is convinced that the transmission of race results can be delayed long enough for him to bet on the winner after the race has been run. He is fleeced when an insideman gives him an erroneous message.

A Directory of Consumer Protection Agencies

(WHOM TO CALL WHEN YOU'RE SUSPICIOUS OR WHEN YOU HAVEN'T BEEN SUSPICIOUS ENOUGH)

Alabama

State Offices
- (1) Governor's Office
  Director of Consumer Protection
  138 Adams Avenue
  Montgomery, Alabama 36130
  (205) 832-5936
  (800) 392-5658

- (2) Consumer Services Director
  Office of Attorney General
  669 South Lawrence Street
  Montgomery, Alabama 36104
  (205) 834-5150

- (3) State Securities Commission
  100 Commerce Street
  Southern Federal Tower
  Suite 1000
  Montgomery, Alabama 36130
  (205) 832-5733

Federal Information Centers
  Birmingham   (205) 322-8591
  Mobile   (205) 438-1421

Alaska

State Offices
(1) Consumer Protection Section
    Office of Attorney General
    420 L Street, Suite 100
    Anchorage, Alaska 99501
    (907) 279-0428

(2) Consumer Protection Section
    State Court Office Building
    604 Barnette, Room 228
    Fairbanks, Alaska 99707
    (907) 465-3692

(3) Consumer Protection Section
    Pouch K. Room 1568
    State Capitol
    Juneau, Alaska 99811
    (907) 465-3692

(4) State Securities Commission
    Division of Banking and Securities
    Pouch D
    Juneau, Alaska 99811
    (907) 465-2521

Arizona

State Offices
(1) Economic Protection Division
    100 North Stone Avenue, Suite 1004
    Tucson, Arizona 85701
    (602) 882-5501

(2) State Securities Commission
    2222 West Encanto Blvd.
    Phoenix, Arizona 85009
    (602) 255-4242

Federal Information Centers
    Phoenix   (602) 261-3313
    Tucson   (602) 622-1511

Arkansas

State Offices
  (1) Deputy Attorney General
      Consumer Protection Division
      Justice Building
      Little Rock, Arkansas 72201
      (501) 371-2341
      (800) 482-8982 (Arkansas only)

  (2) State Securities Commission
      Suite 4B206
      1 Capitol Mall
      Little Rock, Arkansas 72201
      (501) 371-1011

Federal Information Center
  Little Rock   (501) 378-6177

California

State Offices
  (1) Public Inquiry Unit
      Office of Attorney General
      555 Capitol Mall
      Sacramento, California 95814
      (916) 322-3360

  (2) California Department of Consumer Affairs
      1020 North Street
      Sacramento, California 95814
      (916) 445-0660   (complaint mediation)
      (916) 445-1254   (consumer information)
      (800) 366-5131   (auto repair complaints, California only)

  (3) California Department of Consumer Affairs
      107 South Broadway, Room 8020
      Los Angeles, California 90012
      (213) 620-4360

  (4) California Department of Consumer Affairs
      30 VanNess Avenue, Room 2100
      San Francisco, California 94102
      (415) 557-2046

  (5) State Securities Commission
      Department of Corporations
      1025 P Street, Suite 205
      Sacramento, California 95814
      (916) 445-7205

A Directory of Consumer Protection Agencies

(6) State Securities Commission
600 South Commonwealth Avenue
Los Angeles, California 90005
(213) 736-2741

(7) State Securities Commission
600 California Street
San Francisco, California 94108
(415) 557-3787

(8) State Securities Commission
1350 Front Street
San Diego, California 92101
(714) 236-7341

Federal Regional Offices

(1) Securities and Exchange Commission Regional Office
Suite 1710
10960 Wilshire Blvd.
Los Angeles, California 90024
(213) 473-4511

(2) Federal Trade Commission Regional Office
Room 13209
Federal Building
11000 Wilshire Blvd.
Los Angeles, California 90024
(213) 824-7575

(3) Federal Trade Commission Regional Office
450 Golden Gate Avenue
Box 36005
San Francisco, California 94102
(415) 556-1270

(4) Consumer Product Safety Commission Regional Office
3660 Wilshire Blvd., Suite 1100
Los Angeles, California 90010
(213) 688-7272

(5) Consumer Product Safety Commission Regional Office
100 Pine Street, Suite 500
San Francisco, California 94111
(415) 556-1816

Federal Information Centers

Los Angeles	(213) 688-3800
Sacramento	(916) 440-3344
San Diego	(714) 293-6030
San Francisco	(415) 556-6600
San Jose	(408) 275-7422
Santa Ana	(714) 836-2386

Colorado

State Offices
  (1) Consumer Section
      1525 Sherman Street
      4th Floor
      Denver, Colorado 80203
      (303) 839-3611

  (2) Division of Securities
      230 State Office Building
      Denver, Colorado 80203
      (303) 839-2607

Federal Regional Offices
  (1) Securities and Exchange Commission Regional Office
      Room 640
      Two Park Central
      1515 Arapahoe Street
      Denver, Colorado 80202
      (303) 837-2071

  (2) Federal Trade Commission Regional Office
      Suite 2900
      1405 Curtis Street
      Denver, Colorado 80202
      (303) 837-2271

  (3) Consumer Product Safety Commission Regional Office
      Guaranty Bank Building, Suite 938
      817 17th Street
      Denver, Colorado 80202
      (303) 837-2904

Federal Information Centers
  Colorado Springs   (303) 471-9491
  Denver   (303) 837-3602
  Pueblo   (303) 544-9523

Connecticut

State Offices
  (1) Commissioner
      Department of Consumer Protection
      State Office Building
      Hartford, Connecticut 06115
      (203) 566-4999
      (800) 842-2649 (Connecticut only)

(2) State Securities Commission
State Office Building
Hartford, Connecticut 06115
(203) 566-5948
(203) 566-5949 (Director of Broker-Dealer Regulations)
(203) 566-4216 (Director of Securities Enforcement and Registration)
(203) 566-7580 (Banking Commissioner)
(203) 566-5948 (Associate Examiner, Broker-Dealer and Investment Adviser Registrations and Examinations)

Federal Information Centers
Hartford   (203) 527-2617
New Haven (203) 624-4720

Delaware

State Offices
(1) Director
Consumer Affairs Division
Department of Community Affairs and Economic Development
820 North French Street, 4th Floor
Wilmington, Delaware 19801
(302) 571-3250

(2) Division of Securities
State Office Building
820 North French Street
8th Floor
Wilmington, Delaware 19801
(302) 571-2515

District of Columbia

State Offices
(1) Director
D. C. Office of Consumer Protection
1424 K Street, N.W.
Washington, D. C. 20005
(202) 727-1158

(2) State Securities Commission
1625 I Street, N.W.
Washington, D. C. 20006
(202) 727-3006

Federal Information Center
Washington   (202) 755-8660

Florida

State Offices
   (1) Director
       Division of Consumer Services
       110 Mayo Building
       Tallahassee, Florida 32304
       (904) 488-2221
       (800) 342-2176 (Florida only)

   (2) Consumer Counsel
       Consumer Protection and Fair Trade Practices Bureau
       Department of Legal Affairs
       State Capitol
       Tallahassee, Florida 32304
       (904) 488-8916

   (3) Assistant Attorney General
       Dade County Regional Service Center
       401 NW 2nd Avenue, Suite 820
       Miami, Florida 33128
       (305) 377-5441

   (4) Assistant Attorney General
       Division of Consumer Services
       1313 Tampa Street, 8th Floor
       Park Trammell
       Tampa, Florida 33602
       (813) 272-2670

   (5) Division of Securities
       Department of Banking and Finance
       1402 The Capitol
       Tallahassee, Florida 32304
       (904) 488-9805

Federal Information Centers
   Fort Lauderdale   (305) 522-8531
   Jacksonville   (904) 354-4756
   Miami   (305) 350-4155
   Orlando   (305) 422-1800
   St. Petersburg   (813) 893-3495
   Tampa   (813) 229-7911
   West Palm Beach   (305) 833-7566

Georgia

State Offices
  (1) Administrator
      Governor's Office of Consumer Affairs
      225 Peachtree Street, N.E.
      Suite 400
      Atlanta, Georgia 30303
      (404) 656-4900
      (800) 282-4900

  (2) Department of Deceptive Practices
      Office of Attorney General
      132 State Judicial Building
      Atlanta, Georgia 30334
      (404) 656-3391

  (3) Office of Secretary of State
      Division of Securities
      214 State Capitol
      Atlanta, Georgia 30334
      (404) 656-2894

Federal Regional Offices
  (1) Securities and Exchange Commission Regional Office
      Suite 788
      1375 Peachtree Street, N.E.
      Atlanta, Georgia 30309
      (404) 881-4768

  (2) Federal Trade Commission Regional Office
      Room 1000
      1718 Peachtree Street, N.W.
      Atlanta, Georgia 30309
      (404) 881-4836

  (3) Consumer Product Safety Commission Regional Office
      1330 West Peachtree Street, N.W.
      Atlanta, Georgia 30309
      (404) 881-2231

Federal Information Center
   Atlanta   (404) 221-6891

Hawaii

State Offices
  (1) Director of Consumer Protection
     Office of the Governor
     250 South King Street
     P.O. Box 3767
     Honolulu, Hawaii 96811
     (800) 548-2560   (administrative and legal office)
     (800) 548-2540   (complaints)

  (2) Commissioner of Securities
     Department of Regulatory Agencies
     P.O. Box 40
     Honolulu, Hawaii 96810
     (808) 548-7505

Federal Information Center
  Honolulu   (808) 546-8620

Idaho

State Offices
  (1) Deputy Attorney General
     Consumer Protection Division
     State Capitol
     Boise, Idaho 83720
     (208) 384-2400
     (800) 632-5937

  (2) State Securities Commission
     Statehouse Mall
     Boise, Idaho 83720
     (208) 334-3684
     (208) 334-3313   (Director of Finance)
     (208) 334-3684   (Bureau Chief, Securities Bureau)

Illinois

State Offices
  (1) Special Assistant to the Governor
     Consumer Advocate Office
     Office of the Governor
     160 North LaSalle Street, Room 2010
     Chicago, Illinois 60601
     (312) 793-2754

(2) Consumer Fraud Section
　　Office of Attorney General
　　228 North LaSalle Street, Room 1242
　　Chicago, Illinois 60601
　　(312) 793-3580

(3) Special Assistant to the Attorney General
　　Consumer Fraud Section
　　2151 Madison
　　Bellwood, Illinois 60104
　　(312) 344-7700

(4) Special Assistant to the Attorney General
　　Consumer Fraud Section
　　500 Raupp Blvd.
　　Buffalo Grove, Illinois 60090
　　(312) 459-2500 (Saturday only)

(5) Special Assistant to the Attorney General
　　Consumer Fraud Section
　　1104 North Ashland Avenue
　　Chicago, Illinois 60622
　　(312) 793-5638

(6) Consumer Fraud Section
　　13051 Grainwood Avenue
　　Blue Island, Illinois 60406
　　(312) 597-5531

(7) Special Assistant to the Attorney General
　　Consumer Fraud Section
　　4750 North Broadway, Room 216
　　Chicago, Illinois 60640
　　(312) 769-3742

(8) Special Assistant to the Attorney General
　　Consumer Fraud Section
　　800 Lee Street
　　DesPlaines, Illinois 60016
　　(312) 824-4200 (Saturday only)

(9) Special Assistant to the Attorney General
　　Consumer Fraud Section
　　Evanston Library
　　1703 Orrington
　　Evanston, Illinois 60204
　　(312) 866-0300

(10) Special Assistant to the Attorney General
Consumer Fraud Section
P.O. Box 752
71 North Ottawa Street
Joliet, Illinois 60434
(815) 727-3019

(11) Special Assistant to the Attorney General
Consumer Fraud Section
6250 North Lincoln Avenue
Morton Grove, Illinois 60050
(312) 965-5030 (Saturday only)

(12) Consumer Fraud Section
162 Lakehurst
Waukegan, Illinois 60085
(312) 473-3302 (Saturday only)

(13) Special Assistant to the Attorney General
Consumer Fraud Section
1000 Schaumburg Road
Schaumburg, Illinois 60172
(312) 884-7710

(14) Special Assistant to the Attorney General
Consumer Fraud Section
5127 Oakton Street
Skokie, Illinois 60077
(312) 674-2522

(15) Assistant Attorney and Chief Consumer Protection Division
Office of Attorney General
500 South Second Street
Springfield, Illinois 62706
(217) 782-9011

(16) Special Assistant to the Attorney General
Consumer Fraud Section
103 South Washington, Suite 12
Carbondale, Illinois 62901
(618) 457-7831

(17) Special Assistant to the Attorney General
Consumer Fraud Section
818 Martin Luther King Drive
St. Louis, Illinois 62201
(618) 874-2238

(18) Special Assistant to the Attorney General
Consumer Fraud Section
500 Main Street
Peoria, Illinois 61602
(309) 671-3191

(19) Special Assistant to the Attorney General
Consumer Fraud Section
208 18th Street
Rock Island, Illinois 61201
(309) 786-3303

(20) Special Assistant to the Attorney General
Consumer Fraud Section
301 Rockriver Savings Building
Rockford, Illinois 61101
(815) 968-1881

(21) Office of Secretary of State
Securities Division
296 Centennial Building
Springfield, Illinois 62756
(217) 782-2256

Federal Regional Offices
(1) Securities and Exchange Commission Regional Office
Room 1204
Everett McKinley Dirksen Building
219 South Dearborn Street
Chicago, Illinois 60604
(312) 353-7390

(2) Commodity Futures Trading Commission Regional Office
233 South Wacker Drive
46th Floor
Chicago, Illinois 60606
(312) 353-6642

(3) Federal Trade Commission Regional Office
Suite 1437
55 East Monroe Street
Chicago, Illinois 60603
(312) 353-4423

(4) Consumer Product Safety Commission Regional Office
230 South Dearborn Street
Room 2945
Chicago, Illinois 60604
(312) 353-8260

Federal Information Center
Chicago   (312) 353-4242

Indiana

State Offices
  (1) Director
     Consumer Protection Division
     Office of Attorney General
     215 State House
     Indianapolis, Indiana 46204
     (317) 633-6496, 6276
     (800) 382-5516

  (2) State Securities Commission
     102 State House
     Indianapolis, Indiana 46204
     (317) 232-6681

Federal Information Centers
  Gary/Hammond   (219) 883-4110
  Indianapolis   (317) 269-7373

Iowa

State Offices
  (1) Assistant Attorney General in Charge
     Consumer Protection Division
     Office of Attorney General
     1300 East Walnut
     Des Moines, Iowa 50319
     (515) 281-5926

  (2) State Securities Commission
     Lucas State Office Building
     Des Moines, Iowa 50319
     (515) 281-4441

Federal Information Center
  Des Moines   (515) 284-4448

Kansas

State Offices
  (1) Assistant Attorney General
     Consumer Protection Division
     Office of Attorney General
     Kansas Judicial Center
     301 West 10th, 2nd Floor
     Topeka, Kansas 66612
     (913) 296-3751

(2) State Securities Commission
109 West 9th
Suite 501
Topeka, Kansas 66612
(913) 296-3307

Federal Information Centers
Topeka   (913) 295-2866
Wichita (316) 263-6931

Kentucky

State Offices
(1) Assistant Deputy Attorney General
Consumer Protection Division
Executive Building
209 St. Clair Street
Frankfort, Kentucky 40601
(502) 564-6607
(800) 372-2960

(2) State Securities Commission
911 Leawood Drive
Frankfort, Kentucky 40601
(502) 564-2180

Federal Information Center
Louisville   (502) 582-6261

Louisiana

State Offices
(1) State Director
Consumer Protection Section
Office of Attorney General
1885 Wooddale Blvd., Suite 1208
Baton Rouge, Louisiana 70806
(504) 925-4181

(2) Southern Regional Director
Consumer Protection Section
234 Loyola Avenue, 7th Floor
New Orleans, Louisiana 70112
(504) 568-5575

(3) State Securities Commission
315 Louisiana State Office Building
New Orleans, Louisiana 70112
(504) 568-5515

Federal Information Center
New Orleans   (504) 589-6696

Maine

State Offices
(1) Assistant Attorney General
    Consumer and Antitrust Division
    505 State Office Building
    Augusta, Maine 04333
    (207) 289-3716

(2) Deputy Superintendent
    Bureau of Consumer Protection
    State House Station 35
    Augusta, Maine 04333
    (207) 289-3731

(3) State Securities Commission
    State and House Station 36
    Augusta, Maine 04333
    (207) 289-2261

Maryland

State Offices
(1) Consumer Protection Division
    Office of Attorney General
    131 East Redwood Street
    Baltimore, Maryland 21202
    (301) 383-5344

(2) Consumer Specialist
    Maryland Attorney General's Consumer Protection Division
    5112 Berwyn Road, 3rd Floor
    College Park, Maryland 20740
    (301) 474-3500

(3) Director
    Maryland Attorney General's Consumer Protection Division
    138 East Antietam Street
    Hagerstown, Maryland 21740
    (301) 791-4780

(4) State Securities Commission
    Room 602
    26 South Calvert Street
    Baltimore, Maryland 21202
    (301) 383-3714

Federal Information Center
   Baltimore   (301) 962-4980

Massachusetts

State Offices
- (1) Consumer Protection Division
    Department of Attorney General
    One Ashburton Place, 19th Floor
    Boston, Massachusetts 02108
    (617) 727-8400

- (2) Assistant Attorney General for Consumer Protection
    235 Chestnut Street
    Springfield, Massachusetts 01103
    (413) 785-1951

- (3) The Commonwealth of Massachusetts
    Secretary of the Commonwealth
    Securities Division
    John W. McCormack Building
    Room 1719
    One Ashburton Place
    Boston, Massachusetts 02108
    (617) 727-3548

Federal Regional Offices
- (1) Securities and Exchange Commission Regional Office
    150 Causeway Street
    Boston, Massachusetts 02114
    (617) 223-2721

- (2) Federal Trade Commission Regional Office
    Room 1301
    150 Causeway Street
    Boston, Massachusetts 02114
    (617) 223-6621

- (3) Consumer Product Safety Commission Regional Office
    100 Summer Street
    16th Floor, Room 1607
    Boston, Massachusetts 02110
    (617) 223-5576

Federal Information Center
    Boston   (617) 223-7121

Michigan

State Offices
- (1) Assistant Attorney General
    Consumer Protection Division
    690 Law Building
    Lansing, Michigan 48913
    (517) 373-1140

(2) Executive Director
Michigan Consumers Council
414 Hollister Building
106 North Allegan Street
Lansing, Michigan 48933
(517) 373-0947
(800) 292-5680

(3) Corporation and Securities Bureau
Department of Commerce
P.O. Box 30222
6546 Mercantile Way
Lansing, Michigan 48909
(517) 374-9417

Federal Information Centers
Detroit   (313) 226-7016
Grand Rapids   (616) 451-2628

Minnesota

State Offices
(1) Special Assistant to the Attorney General
Consumer Protection Division
102 State Capitol
St. Paul, Minnesota 55155
(612) 296-3353

(2) Office of Consumer Services
7th and Robert Streets
St. Paul, Minnesota 55101
(612) 296-4512
(612) 296-2331 (complaints)

(3) Office of Consumer Services
Duluth Regional Office
604 Alworth Building
Duluth, Minnesota 55802
(218) 723-4891

(4) State Securities Commission
500 Metro Square Building
St. Paul, Minnesota 55101
(612) 296-2594

Federal Regional Offices
(1) Commodity Futures Trading Commission
Regional Office
510 Grain Exchange Building
Minneapolis, Minnesota 55415
(612) 725-2025

(2) Consumer Product Safety Commission
Regional Office
Metro Square, Suite 580
7th and Robert Streets
St. Paul, Minnesota 55101
(612) 725-7781

Federal Information Center
Minneapolis   (612) 725-2073

Mississippi

State Offices
(1) Consumer Protection Division
Office of Attorney General
Justice Building
P.O. Box 220
Jackson, Mississippi 39205
(601) 354-7130

(2) State Securities Commission
106 State Executive Building
P.O. Box 136
Jackson, Mississippi 39205
(601) 354-6548

Missouri

State Offices
(1) Chief Counsel
Consumer Protection Division
Office of Attorney General
Supreme Court Building
P.O. Box 899
Jefferson City, Missouri 65102
(314) 751-3321

(2) Consumer Protection Division
Office of Attorney General
705 Olive Street
Suite 1323
St. Louis, Missouri 63101
(314) 241-2211

(3) Consumer Protection Division
Office of Attorney General
615 East 13th Street
Kansas City, Missouri 64106
(816) 274-6686

(4) State Securities Commission
    State Capitol Building
    Jefferson City, Missouri 65102
    (314) 751-4136

Federal Regional Offices
(1) Commodity Futures Trading Commission
    Regional Office
    4901 Main Street
    Room 208
    Kansas City, Missouri 64112
    (816) 374-2994

(2) Consumer Product Safety Commission
    Regional Office
    Traders National Bank Building
    Suite 1500
    1125 Grand Avenue
    Kansas City, Missouri 64106
    (816) 374-2034

Federal Information Centers
    Kansas City   (816) 374-2466
    St. Joseph   (816) 233-8206
    St. Louis   (314) 425-4106

Montana

State Offices
(1) Administrator
    Consumer Affairs Division
    Department of Business Regulation
    805 North Main Street
    Helena, Montana 59601
    (406) 449-3163

(2) State Securities Commission
    Mitchell Building
    Helena, Montana 59601
    (406) 449-2040

Nebraska

State Offices
(1) Attorney General
    Consumer Protection Division
    State House
    Lincoln, Nebraska 68509
    (402) 471-2682

(2) State Securities Commission
301 Centennial Mall South
P.O. Box 95006
Lincoln, Nebraska 68509
(402) 471-3445

Federal Information Center
Omaha   (402) 221-3353

Nevada

State Offices
(1) Deputy Attorney General
Consumer Affairs Division
2501 East Sahara Avenue
3rd Floor
Las Vegas, Nevada 89158
(702) 386-5293

(2) Deputy Commissioner
Consumer Affairs Division
Department of Commerce
201 Nye Building
Capitol Complex
Carson City, Nevada 89710
(702) 885-4340
(800) 992-0973

(3) State Securities Commission
State Capitol
Carson City, Nevada 89710
(702) 885-5203

New Hampshire

State Offices
(1) Chief
Consumer Protection Antitrust Division
Office of Attorney General
State House Annex
Concord, New Hampshire 03301
(603) 271-3641

(2) State Securities Commission
169 Manchester Street
Concord, New Hampshire 03301
(603) 271-2261

New Jersey

State Offices
 (1) Director
    Division of Consumer Affairs
    Department of Law and Public Safety
    1100 Raymond Blvd., Room 504
    Newark, New Jersey 07102
    (201) 648-4010

 (2) Deputy Commissioner
    Division of Consumer Complaints
    Legal and Economic Research
    P.O. Box CN040
    Trenton, New Jersey 08625
    (609) 292-5341

 (3) State Securities Commission
    80 Mulberry Street
    Room 308
    Newark, New Jersey 07102
    (201) 648-2040

Federal Information Centers
 Newark   (201) 645-3600
 Paterson/Passaic (201) 523-0717
 Trenton   (609) 396-4400

New Mexico

State Offices
 (1) Director
    Consumer and Economic Crime Division
    Office of Attorney General
    P.O. Box 1508
    Santa Fe, New Mexico 87501
    (505) 827-5521

 (2) Securities Bureau
    Lew Wallace Building
    Santa Fe, New Mexico 87503
    (505) 827-5368

Federal Information Centers
 Albuquerque (505) 766-3091
 Santa Fe   (505) 983-7743

New York

State Offices
- (1) Assistant Attorney General in Charge
    Consumer Frauds and Protection Bureau
    Office of Attorney General
    Two World Trade Center
    New York, New York 10047
    (212) 488-7450

- (2) Assistant Attorney General
    Consumer Frauds and Protection Bureau
    State Capitol
    Albany, New York 12224
    (518) 474-8686

- (3) Assistant Attorney General in Charge
    10 Lower Metcalf Plaza
    Auburn, New York 13021
    (315) 253-9765

- (4) Assistant Attorney General in Charge
    Office of Attorney General
    44 Hawley Street
    State Office Building
    Binghampton, New York 13901
    (607) 773-7823

- (5) Assistant Attorney General in Charge
    Office of Attorney General
    65 Court Street
    Buffalo, New York 14202
    (716) 842-4396

- (6) Assistant Attorney General in Charge
    Suffolk State Office Building
    Veterans Memorial Highway
    Hauppauge, New York 11787
    (516) 979-5190

- (7) Assistant Attorney General in Charge
    Office of Attorney General
    48 Cornelia Street
    Plattsburgh, New York 12901
    (518) 561-1980

- (8) Assistant Attorney General
    Office of Attorney General
    65 Broad Street
    Rochester, New York 14614
    (716) 454-4540

(9) Acting Assistant Attorney General in Charge
333 East Washington Street
Syracuse, New York 13202
(315) 473-8181

(10) Assistant Attorney General
40 Garden Street
Poughkeepsie, New York 12601
(914) 452-7744

(11) Assistant Attorney General in Charge
207 Genesee Street, Box 528
Utica, New York 13501
(315) 797-6120, Ext. 234

(12) Assistant Attorney General in Charge
317 Washington Street
Watertown, New York 13601
(315) 782-0100, Ext. 444

(13) State Securities Commission
Two World Trade Center
New York, New York 10047
(212) 488-3310

Federal Regional Offices
(1) Securities and Exchange Commission
Regional Office
26 Federal Plaza, Room 1102
New York, New York 10007
(212) 264-1636

(2) Commodity Futures Trading Commission
Regional Office
One World Trade Center
Suite 4747
New York, New York 10048
(212) 446-2068

(3) Federal Trade Commission
Regional Office
2443-EB, Federal Building
26 Federal Plaza
New York, New York 10007
(212) 264-1207

(4) Consumer Product Safety Commission
Regional Office
6 World Trade Center
Vesey Street, 6th Floor
New York, New York 10048
(212) 264-1125

Federal Information Centers
  Albany   (518) 463-4421
  Buffalo   (716) 846-4010
  New York   (212) 264-4464
  Rochester   (716) 546-5075
  Syracuse   (315) 476-8545

North Carolina

State Offices
  (1) Consumer Protection Division
      Justice Building, P.O. Box 629
      Raleigh, North Carolina 27602
      (919) 733-7741

  (2) State Securities Commission
      101 The Administration Building
      Raleigh, North Carolina 27611
      (919) 733-3433
      (919) 733-3924 (Securities Deputy)

Federal Information Center
  Charlotte   (704) 376-3600

North Dakota

State Offices
  (1) Assistant Attorney General and Counsel
      Consumer Fraud Division
      State Capitol Building
      Bismarck, North Dakota 58505
      (701) 224-3404
      (800) 472-2600 (North Dakota residents only)

  (2) State Securities Commission
      State Capitol
      Bismarck, North Dakota 58505
      (701) 224-2910

Ohio

State Offices
  (1) Assistant Attorney General and Section Chief
      Consumer Frauds and Crimes Section
      30 East Broad Street
      Columbus, Ohio 43215
      (614) 466-8831

(2) State Securities Commission
180 East Broad Street
Columbus, Ohio 43215
(614) 466-3440
(614) 466-7602 (Commissioner of Securities)

Federal Regional Offices
(1) Federal Trade Commission
Regional Office
Suite 500
Mall Building
118 St. Clair Avenue
Cleveland, Ohio 44144
(216) 522-4207

(2) Consumer Product Safety Commission
Regional Office
Plaza 9 Building, Suite 520
55 Erieview Plaza, 5th Floor
Cleveland, Ohio 44114
(216) 522-3886

Federal Information Centers
Akron   (216) 375-5638
Cincinnati   (513) 684-2801
Cleveland   (216) 522-4040
Columbus   (614) 221-1014
Dayton   (513) 223-7377
Toledo   (419) 241-3223

Oklahoma

State Offices
(1) Administrator
Department of Consumer Affairs
460 Jim Thorpe Building
Oklahoma City, Oklahoma 73105
(415) 521-3653

(2) Assistant Attorney General for Consumer Protection
112 State Capitol Building
Oklahoma City, Oklahoma 73105
(405) 521-3921

(3) State Securities Commission
2915 North Lincoln
Oklahoma City, Oklahoma 73105
(405) 521-2451

Federal Information Centers
   Oklahoma City   (405) 231-4868
   Tulsa   (918) 584-4193

Oregon

State Offices
   (1) Chief Counsel
       Consumer Protection Division
       Office of Attorney General
       520 SW Yamhill Street
       Portland, Oregon 97204
       (503) 229-5522

   (2) Consumer Services Division
       Department of Commerce
       Labor and Industries Building
       Salem, Oregon 97310
       (503) 378-4320

   (3) Department of Commerce
       Corporation Division
       158-12th Street, N.E.
       Salem, Oregon 97310
       (503) 378-4387

Federal Information Center
   Portland   (503) 221-2222

Pennsylvania

State Offices
   (1) Bureau of Consumer Protection
       301 Market Street, 9th Floor
       Harrisburg, Pennsylvania 17101
       (717) 787-9707

   (2) Deputy Attorney General
       Bureau of Consumer Protection
       Department of Justice
       133 North 5th Street
       Allentown, Pennsylvania 18102
       (215) 821-0901

   (3) Assistant Attorney General
       Bureau of Consumer Protection
       Department of Justice
       919 State Street, Room 203
       Erie, Pennsylvania 16501
       (814) 871-4371

(4) Bureau of Consumer Protection
Department of Justice
Strawberry Square, 15th Floor
Harrisburg, Pennsylvania 17121
(717) 787-7109

(5) Attorney General
1405 Locust Street, Suite 825
Philadelphia, Pennsylvania 19102
(215) 238-6475

(6) Attorney General
Bureau of Consumer Protection
Department of Justice
300 Liberty Avenue, Room 1405
Pittsburgh, Pennsylvania 15222
(412) 565-5135

(7) Deputy Attorney General
Bureau of Consumer Protection
Department of Justice
100 Lackawanna Avenue
105A State Office Building
Scranton, Pennsylvania 18503
(717) 961-4913

(8) State Securities Commission
471 Education Building
Harrisburg, Pennsylvania 17120
(717) 787-8061

Federal Regional Offices
(1) Consumer Product Safety Commission
Regional Office
400 Market Street, 10th Floor
Philadelphia, Pennsylvania 19106
(215) 597-9105

Federal Information Centers
Allentown/Bethlehem	(215) 821-7785
Philadelphia	(215) 597-7042
Pittsburgh	(412) 644-3456
Scranton	(717) 346-7081

Puerto Rico

Government Offices
  (1) Department of Consumer Affairs
      Minillas Governmental Center
      Torre Norte Building
      De Diego Avenue, Stop 22
      P.O. Box 41059
      Santurce, Puerto Rico 00940
      (809) 726-6090

  (2) Department of Treasury
      P.O. Box S-4515
      San Juan, Puerto Rico 00905
      (809) 725-1616
      (809) 725-4075, Ext. 380 (Director, Bureau of Securities)

Rhode Island

State Offices
  (1) Public Protection Consumer Unit
      Department of Attorney General
      56 Pine Street
      Providence, Rhode Island 02903
      (401) 277-3163

  (2) State Securities Commission
      100 North Main Street
      Providence, Rhode Island 02903
      (401) 277-2405

Federal Information Center
   Providence   (401) 331-5565

South Carolina

State Offices
  (1) Department of Consumer Affairs
      2221 Devine Street
      Columbia, South Carolina 29211
      (803) 758-2040
      (800) 922-1594

  (2) Assistant Attorney General for Consumer Protection
      2303 Devine Street
      Columbia, South Carolina 29205
      (803) 758-3040

(3) State Securities Commission
816 Keenan Building
Columbia, South Carolina 29201
(803) 758-2833

South Dakota

State Offices
(1) Assistant Attorney General
Division of Consumer Protection
Capitol Building
Pierre, South Dakota 57501
(605) 773-3215

(2) Office of the Attorney General
Division of Consumer Protection
114 South Main Avenue
Sioux Falls, South Dakota 57102
(605) 339-6691

(3) State Securities Commission
Capitol Building
Pierre, South Dakota 57501
(605) 773-3177

Tennessee

State Offices
(1) Assistant Attorney General for Consumer Protection
450 James Robertson Parkway
Nashville, Tennessee 37219
(615) 741-1671

(2) Loans and Securities Division
Department of Insurance
114 State Office Building
Nashville, Tennessee 37219
(615) 741-2947

Federal Information Centers
  Chattanooga   (615) 265-8231
  Memphis   (901) 521-3285
  Nashville   (615) 242-5056

Texas

State Offices
(1) Assistant Attorney General
Consumer Protection and Antitrust Division
Office of Attorney General
P.O. Box 12548, Capitol Station
Austin, Texas 78711
(512) 475-3288

(2) Assistant Attorney General
Consumer Protection Division
4313 North 10th, Suite F
McAllen, Texas 78501
(512) 682-4547

(3) Assistant Attorney General
Consumer Protection Division
701 Commerce, Suite 200
Dallas, Texas 75202
(214) 742-8944

(4) Assistant Attorney General
Consumer Protection Division
4824 Alberta Avenue
Suite 160
El Paso, Texas 79905
(915) 533-3484

(5) Assistant Attorney General
Consumer Protection Division
312 County Office Building
806 Broadway
Lubbock, Texas 79401
(806) 747-5238

(6) Assistant Attorney General
Consumer Protection Division
200 Main Plaza, Suite 400
San Antonio, Texas 78205
(512) 225-4191

(7) Assistant Attorney General
Consumer Protection Division
723 Main Street, Suite 610
Houston, Texas 77002
(713) 228-0701

(8) State Securities Commission
P.O. Box 13167
Capitol Station
Austin, Texas 78711
(512) 474-2233

Federal Regional Offices
(1) Securities and Exchange Commission
Regional Office
8th Floor
411 West Seventh Street
Fort Worth, Texas 76102
(817) 334-3393

(2) Federal Trade Commission
Regional Office
Suite 2665
2001 Bryan Street
Dallas, Texas 75201
(214) 729-0032

(3) Consumer Product Safety Commission
Regional Office
500 South Ervay, Room 410C
Dallas, Texas 75201
(214) 749-3871

Federal Information Centers
Austin	(512) 472-5494
Dallas	(214) 767-8585
Fort Worth	(817) 334-3624
Houston	(713) 226-5711
San Antonio	(512) 224-4471

Utah

State Offices
(1) Division of Consumer Affairs
Utah Trade Commission Department of Business Regulation
330 East Fourth Street
Salt Lake City, Utah 84111
(801) 533-6441

(2) Assistant Attorney General
Consumer Protection Unit
Office of Attorney General
236 State Capitol
Salt Lake City, Utah 84114
(801) 533-5261

(3) State Securities Commission
   330 East 4th South
   Salt Lake City, Utah 84111
   (801) 533-4239

Federal Information Centers
   Ogden   (801) 399-1347
   Salt Lake City   (801) 524-5353

Vermont

State Offices
   (1) Office of Attorney General
       Consumer Protection Division
       109 State Street
       Montpelier, Vermont 05602
       (802) 828-3171
       (800) 642-5149

   (2) State Securities Commission
       State Office Building
       Montpelier, Vermont 05602
       (802) 828-3301

Virginia

State Offices
   (1) Assistant Attorney General
       Division of Consumer Counsel
       11 South 12th Street, Suite 308
       Richmond, Virginia 23219
       (804) 786-4075

   (2) State Office of Consumer Affairs
       Department of Agriculture and Consumer Services
       825 East Broad Street, Box 1163
       Richmond, Virginia 23209
       (804) 786-2042
       (800) 552-9963 (regarding state agencies)

   (3) Office of Consumer Affairs
       3016 Williams Drive
       Fairfax, Virginia 22031
       (703) 573-1286

   (4) State Securities Commission
       11 South 12th Street
       Richmond, Virginia 23219
       (804) 786-7751
       (804) 786-7752

Federal Regional Office
(1) Securities and Exchange Commission
    Regional Office
    Ballston Center Tower 3
    4015 Wilson Blvd.
    Arlington, Virginia 22203
    (703) 557-8201

Federal Information Centers
    Newport News   (804) 244-0480
    Norfolk   (804) 441-3101
    Richmond   (804) 643-4928
    Roanoke   (703) 982-8591

Washington

State Offices
(1) Assistant Attorney General
    Consumer Protection Division
    1366 Dexter Horton Building
    Seattle, Washington 98104
    (206) 464-7744
    (800) 552-0700

(2) Consumer Protection Division
    Temple of Justice
    Olympia, Washington 98504
    (206) 753-6210

(3) Spokane Office of Attorney General
    Consumer Protection Division
    960 Paulsen Professional Building
    Spokane, Washington 99201
    (509) 456-3123

(4) Office of Attorney General
    Consumer Protection Division
    620 Perkins Building
    Tacoma, Washington 98402
    (206) 593-2904

(5) Securities Division
    Business and Professions Administration
    P.O. Box 648
    Olympia, Washington 98504
    (206) 753-6928

Federal Regional Offices
  (1) Securities and Exchange Commission
      Regional Office
      3040 Federal Building
      915 Second Avenue
      Seattle, Washington 98174
      (206) 442-7990

  (2) Federal Trade Commission
      Regional Office
      28th Floor
      Federal Building
      915 Second Avenue
      Seattle, Washington 98174
      (206) 442-4655

  (3) Consumer Product Safety Commission
      Regional Office
      3240 Federal Building
      915 Second Avenue
      Seattle, Washington 98174
      (206) 442-5276

Federal Information Centers
  Seattle   (206) 442-0570
  Tacoma   (206) 383-5230

West Virginia

State Offices
  (1) Consumer Protection Division
      Office of Attorney General
      3412 Staunton Avenue, S.E.
      Charleston, West Virginia 25305
      (304) 348-8986

  (2) State Securities Commission
      Room 205-W
      State Capitol Building
      Charleston, West Virginia 25305
      (304) 348-2257

Wisconsin

State Offices
  (1) Assistant Attorney General
      Office of Consumer Protection
      Department of Justice
      State Capitol
      Madison, Wisconsin 53702
      (608) 266-1852

(2) Office of Consumer Protection
Milwaukee State Office Building
819 North 6th Street, Room 520
Milwaukee, Wisconsin 53203
(414) 224-1867

(3) Division of Consumer Protection
P.O. Box 8911
Madison, Wisconsin 53708
(608) 266-9837
(800) 362-8025 (Wisconsin only)

(4) Division of Consumer Affairs
Northwest District Office
1727 Loring Street
Altoona, Wisconsin 54720
(715) 836-2861

(5) Division of Consumer Affairs
Northeast District Office
1181 A Western Avenue
Green Bay, Wisconsin 54303
(414) 497-4210

(6) Division of Consumer Protection
Southeast District Office
10320 West Silver Spring Drive
Milwaukee, Wisconsin 53225
(414) 257-8966

(7) State Securities Commission
P.O. Box 1768
Madison, Wisconsin 53701
(608) 266-3431

Federal Information Center
Milwaukee   (414) 271-2273

Wyoming

State Offices
  (1) Assistant Attorney General
Consumer Protection Division
123 Capitol Building
Cheyenne, Wyoming 82002
(307) 777-7841

  (2) State Securities Commission
State Capitol Building
Cheyenne, Wyoming 82002
(307) 777-7370

Waynesburg College Library
Waynesburg, Pa.   15370